FIRST LIGHT

4/86

For John and Vicki,

With Love and Good Wishes.

From Ethan

FIRST LIGHT

Sojourns with People of the Outer Hebrides, the Sierra Madre,
the Himalayas, and Other Remote Places

ETHAN HUBBARD

CHELSEA GREEN PUBLISHING COMPANY
Chelsea, Vermont 05038

First printing, February 1986

Library of Congress Cataloging in Publication Data

Hubbard, Ethan, 1941-
First Light.

1. Hubbard, Ethan, 1941-
2. Voyages and travels—1951-
I. Title.
G465.H84 1986 910.4 85-29894
ISBN 0-930031-04-0 (alk. paper)

CONTENTS

PREFACE

In the spring of 1978, nearing my thirty-eighth year and determined to bring a deeper sense of fulfillment into my life, I sold my house and land in northern Vermont and began spending as much time as I possibly could with rural and indigenous people.

For the previous ten years I had worked as the deputy director of the Vermont Historical Society, collecting and preserving artifacts and memorabilia for the Vermont Museum and Library. Whenever I felt overwhelmed by my desk work I checked out of the office with a couple of cameras and a tape recorder to visit interesting Vermonters: loggers, blacksmiths, dairy farmers, back-to-the-landers, former moonshiners and rum-runners. I realized that interviewing and photographing such characters was what I wanted to do with my life. I quit my job at the Historical Society and took off to travel around the U.S. in an old VW bus with my dog and a couple of cameras. It was not, as I look back on it, a sense of disillusionment with being a householder that prompted me to travel as much as some inner need seeking realignment with simple and natural things: things like growing seeds, harvesting food, sleeping on the earth, sharing talk with a friend on a porch, listening to the wind in the trees, enjoying the taste of cold spring water.

I grew up on a farm in New England where simple pleasures had been my birthright, pleasures made stronger and more evident through the love and generosity of a sensitive and caring mother. It was she who taught me most about life—the stars, the wildflowers, the coming of the seasons, the spiritual quality of light on a late November afternoon. In the spring we gathered sap from maples on the hillside and made maple syrup on our old cook stove. In summer we made wooden whistles from willow trees that grew down by the pond. In the fall when the air was crisp and sharp my mother took us down through the woods at night with a lantern to listen for the song of an owl we called Old Brown.

Some thirty years later I found myself seeking out traditional cultures in an effort to reacquaint myself with the things my mother had taught me. My journeying began in my own country with native Americans: Navajos, Apaches, Papagos, Sioux. I traveled to their reservations in my VW bus, with my camping gear stashed beneath my bed. I always managed to find an elder who seemed happy to have me about. In visits that lasted a few minutes, to those that eased into days of sharing, I sat at their feet and asked questions with my heart.

Between 1978 and 1980 I drove the back roads of the U.S., stopping to visit with unique and interesting people who were leading lives very different from mine. I shared coffee with cowboys, danced with the Cajuns after rice harvest, herded cattle with Idaho ranch kids, and brought in stove wood with southern blacks and their mules. It was an America I had forgotten existed—a land of wide open spaces, tiny prairie villages with friendly cafes, church socials, and old-timers enjoying good talk on the street.

In 1980 I began traveling farther afield: to the the Outer Hebrides of Scotland, Mexico's Sierra Madre, Nepal, Guatemala, India's Ladakh region, Australia and New Zealand, the Hudson Bay, and Sri Lanka. I traveled as simply and as economically as I could, with a knapsack, a tent and sleeping bag, light cooking gear, cameras and film, and small gifts to give to people I befriended along the way.

Each country that I traveled to was alluring in its own way. The mountains and deserts, the high steppes and tundra, the islands and moors, the rain-forest jungles all awakened in me a deep sense of appreciation and a fuller understanding of my life. The different cultures proved to be empowering teachers. Each village, each family reflected new ways of living. The Nepalese, for example, can grow a year's supply of food on a plot of ground not much bigger than a house. The Innuits, who smiled when they gave their babies away, taught unconditional love. The native Americans held a reverence for the natural world (Mother Earth, Grandfather Sky, and the Four Directions). The Maoris knew the joy of singing. The Australian Aborigines believed that dreams were more real than the ordinary world. The Scots had learned to accept the weather; the Tibetan

Buddhists, their fate. The Mexicans loved laughter and practical jokes.

Returning home to America after my journey to Sri Lanka in 1984, I went back to the family farm in Connecticut. The knapsack I carried through so many different terrains I put temporarily to rest in the attic. My boots and cooking gear I stashed under my bed. I spent most of my time working on this book, taking afternoon walks along the river with my dog, and sharing evening meals around the kitchen table with my mother.

Last night I took my sleeping bag and went up over the fields in the moonlight to sleep on the hill. It was a beautiful New England summer night. The new moon hung low in the west over the pond, blood-red and cream-colored. Cicadas and tree toads echoed in the swamp. Lightning bugs sparkled in the tall grasses, and the air was sweet with the smell of newly mown hay. Lying in my sleeping bag, I gazed skyward where the Big Dipper and the Milky Way blazed clearly. Remembering so many different nights around the world where the same night skies had befriended me, I found myself over-whelmed with thankfulness for my life. Unable to express it more profoundly, I clasped my hands together in prayer and gave thanks to God for both the going out and the coming home, for the decision to follow my heart.

Ethan Hubbard
Washington, Connecticut
August, 1985

Days and months are the travelers of eternity. So are the years that pass by . . . I myself have been tempted for a long time by the cloud-moving wind— filled with a strong desire to wander. . . I walked through mists and clouds, breathing the thin air of high altitudes and stepping on slippery ice and snow, till at last through a gateway of clouds, as it seemed, to the very paths of the sun and moon, I reached the summit, completely out of breath and nearly frozen to death. Presently the sun went down and the moon rose glistening in the sky.

Basho
The Narrow Road to the Deep North

For my teacher, Richard Clarke

Dawn in the Outer Hebrides

ARDNAMORNIE

Fall 1980. My exploration of the Outer Hebrides started on the Isle of Barra. I spent my first night in an abandoned sixteenth-century Christian convent, sleeping in a fallen-down cattle barn close to the sea. My nearest neighbor, a raw-boned crofter with enormous hands and a craggy head, invited me to share a meal of roast mutton and new potatoes with him and his family. When I said goodnight to the family, he walked with me out to the cattle barn. Along the way we lingered on a wooden bridge and watched the new moon in a tumbling stream and a skein of geese cross the misty night skies.

The next day I took the mail boat, a small craft that plowed through the turbulent seas with ease, to the Isle of South Uist. We landed at the small fishing port of Lochboisdale where I disembarked, shouldered my backpack, and headed west out of town. Several hours later, while napping in sweet-scented ferns along the roadside, I was awakened by an old gentleman in a tweed suit and cap on his way to church. He spoke with a thick Gaelic accent, soft as silk, and asked me where I was going. I told him that I was an American touring the island, and that I hoped to find an old-fashioned village of stone cottages with thatched roofs and good people. The old man pointed his walking stick to the west and spoke unhesitatingly, "Now take this road twelve miles until you come to Eocher, and then go west to Ardnamornie village. And be sure to make the acquaintance of the MacCormick family."

In Ardnamornie I asked several herdsmen driving cattle along the dusty road dressed in baggy trousers and tweed jackets if they could direct me to the MacCormicks'. They did, sucking on their pipes as they argued amongst themselves as to which was the better route. I chose the shortest and the wettest way, passing through waist-

Angus MacCormick with a new pup

2 *Ardnamornie*

deep sloughs and quaking bogs that toppled me. When I drew near to the MacCormick farm—five stone buildings, fences, sheep, cattle, fowl—it looked like some early Celtic settlement. The four MacCormicks came slowly out into the cold drizzling rain to inspect me. When I introduced myself and told them that I had come for a visit, they leapt into action like a wartime rescue team. The old sisters pulled off my boots and socks, and the brothers wrestled with my soaked shirts and backpack. With heroic shouts they brought me hot tea, dry towels, a chair by the fire, and a wee dram of whiskey they called the Grouse.

Later in the evening, over a hearty supper of fresh salt herring, new potatoes, and a sweet carrageen pudding for dessert, the four MacCormicks hovered around me like people who had found an abandoned child on their doorstep. They chattered like magpies during the meal, interrupting each other in Gaelic, trying to find out everything about me and my country. We talked well into the night, and when the mantel clock struck eleven, I said goodnight and made my way with my sleeping bag into the darkness. Angus, the older brother, accompanied me with the lantern, eager to show me a dry place to lay my belongings.

The MacCormicks—Angus, 79; Donald, 67; Marion, 74; and Kate Effie, 56—were a remarkably old-fashioned Scottish family, relics from the Celtic past. They kept sheep and cattle, cut peat upon the moors, put up haycocks of barley and oats, and gathered red seaweed for their carrageen pudding. None of them had ever married, none had traveled much beyond Glasgow, and they all spoke Gaelic as their first language. They lived in their three-hundred-year-old ancestral homestead in Ardnamornie much as their parents and grandparents had.

They seemed happy to have me about, and not long after my arrival they insisted I move my sleeping bag and belongings into the snug hay barn, away from the driving gales and rains that swept in off the Atlantic. The hay barn became my home. At night the wind moaned about the eaves and the rain pelted the thatch with a hissing sting. The night sounds of the sheep and cattle serenaded me and often spooked me, as did a crafty black cat who appeared occasionally on a barn beam overhead.

When not helping the MacCormicks with their daily chores, I often wandered across the moors and up the rugged coastline, visiting with the island people. When I returned at night, cold and wet, the MacCormicks were waiting for me in the kitchen like a clutch of brown hens. They served me hot tea and scones, and a glass of the Grouse to take off the chill. The four of them took great interest in finding out where I had been and who I had visited, often voicing strong opinions. "Ah, Laddie, you mustn't take up with those scallywags. Keep away from them is my advice. Why not go and visit with old Peggy and John MacDonald?"

Sundays were special times with the MacCormicks. We went to church as a family. After the breakfast dishes had been done and the geese and chickens fed, the sisters heated up huge pans of water on the stove for the men to shave with. They pressed our pants and white shirts with an old iron heated on the peat stove, and then they made us march around in a circle as they inspected their handiwork. Kate Effie sometimes took me by the hand and made me pirouette, like some circus dancer—"Ah, handsome as a prince, not like some Gypsy who lives in a hay loft."

I particularly enjoyed our evenings together around the kitchen table. Much of their food came directly from their small farm: mutton, potatoes, carrots, oatmeal bread, fresh salt herring. They said the blessing in Gaelic and began to eat, and the brothers, peeling the skins of the new potatoes with their thick thumbnails, made small neat piles of the skins on the sides of their plates. Kate Effie got up from the table every so often to drop another peat into the stove. She was the pivot around which everything turned. Though nearing sixty, she was like a dancer: in four steps to the stove she kicked the cat sideways with a deft slippered foot, bent down to open the firebox, and sighed as she straightened up again and began to stir gravy in a pan with a whirring right hand. Then, weary from her work, she returned to the table. Her cheeks were red and flushed, the bright color of a freshly skinned hare. She managed to raise a laugh, however, and with sparkling blue eyes asked coyly which one of us three fine gentlemen was going to take her out for fish and chips at the restaurant in town. The brothers kept their noses in their food and continued to peel their potatoes in

Donald John MacClellan

6 *Ardnamornie*

silence, but I could not help but feel that Kate was earnest. After dessert and tea, we sat for hours and shared conversation, the brothers in their armchairs with their pipes, the sisters darning by a lamp at the kitchen table. Sometimes we talked about my home in America, but more often than not we talked about the weather, the news of friends and neighbors, and the price of young lambs at the farm auction at Drimore.

Living at the MacCormicks' brought me into contact with many of the people in the community: the veterinarian, the visiting nurse, the local priest, the Pakistani pack peddler, and an old sea captain who stopped in for a smoke and wee dram of the Grouse. Perhaps the most frequent visitor at the MacCormicks' was an old herdsman by the name of Donald John MacClellan. He was the last of his kind in the village to take his herds of sheep and cattle up onto the great Machair, an endless marshland between the mountains and the sea. Whenever I heard his booming voice inside the house, I scrambled out of my sleeping bag, dressed quickly, and joined in the old man's visit. He talked about things as interesting as anything in a museum, things that he remembered hearing as a boy from the sea captains who sailed to St. Kilda: tales of ghosts and ghouls in the highland glens, legends of the Celts and Vikings. He was a huge, raucus man who walked with a swagger and used a shepherd's cane. He often stopped on his way home from the Machair for a drink with the brothers. They were very fond of him. He always sat in the same chair, his back ramrod straight, his large hands resting on the handle of his cane, and he drank glass after glass of the Grouse and recounted his life. This was our entertainment on many nights.

I looked for the old herdsman on many occasions, asking crofters at the edge of the Machair if they had seen him enter at dawn. Once I found him sitting in an old cellar hole in his oil skins, ruminating in the pouring rain. He was always glad to see me. "John," I would say, "how long have those twelve stepping stones been there to help travelers across the wet part of the track?" "Aye," he droned, "they'll be older than the village, and older still than the castle. It was the Vikings that put them there, and that was a long time ago."

I never visited the old man without food or drink: oat cakes and

Old Francis mowing

8 *Ardnamornie*

cheese, a carrot for his horse, a scrap of meat for his dog, and always the wee dram of whiskey. Sometimes we sat and drank in silence, the howling winds and the driving rain obliterating our voices and making our communion a silent one. He told me that at times like these it was far better to have one drink upon the moor than twenty in a warm hotel.

I was in constant awe of Donald John MacClellan and his solitary life as a shepherd. For from the first light until dusk, year after year, he wandered the barren moors with his herds of sheep and cattle. His life was closely bound up with things simple, natural, and true: wind and rain, light and snow, a bit of warmth from a peat fire, the coming of spring, a speckled egg, dappled light on the frozen marsh grass, the world reflected in a sheep's eye.

Near the MacCormicks' lay an old thatched cottage whose well-kept meadows and stone fences signaled a caring steward of the land. One warm September morning, when I found Kate Effie rummaging in the tall grass for a fresh egg for my breakfast, I asked her who lived there. "Old Francis we call him. He's a bachelor who fishes for the flounder and the salmon in the loch. Go see him. He'll enjoy your visit."

The first time I saw Old Francis he was sharpening his scythe in a low meadow. He stood tall and gangly between two haystacks, the high mountains of Uist rising up behind him, the ebbing tides of Loch Bee but a few hundred yards away. All of one week he had tried to teach me to use the scythe. I was terrible at it, but he did not seem to mind. Mowing grasses down by the loch, watching the arc of the sun in the autumn sky, these were good times for us both, and gave Old Francis a chance to share the stories that spilled out of him.

We dug potatoes together in a meadow that touched the great marshlands to the east. His welty old hands and mine made a strange team on autumn mornings. The potatoes spilled out of their loamy dens like moles and made a pleasing sound as they landed in the white enamel pail. Everyone said that Old Francis grew the best potatoes in Ardnamornie. Even Kate Effie, who had thrown him out on his ear many times when he was drunk, admitted it.

I used to sneak away from the MacCormicks as often as I could to spend time with Old Francis. On cold autumn evenings, when the mist and rain from the Atlantic drove hard against his cottage, I

Kirsti MacLean harvesting fall oats

visited him on my bicycle, soaked, carrying cheese, oat cakes, and a bottle of the Grouse in a small rucksack. We sat by the glowing candle in front of the peat fire, his black lean dogs resting on either side of our chairs, and we talked softly and mournfully as the autumn rain fell outside.

In Cleat Cove, where the curved beach shone white against the dark blue currents of the Gulf Stream, I often went to help an old couple cut and stack their fall oats. John and Kirsti MacLean were delightful, easygoing and fun, appreciative of one another and of their lives upon the land. Kirsti, nearing seventy, enjoyed teaching me how to bundle loose oats in the meadow and how to tie them with a few strands of rye grass. Together, we trudged with enormous loads upon our backs, laughing the entire way back to the barnyard where John would be waiting for us. "Aye, what are you two laughing at now?" he would say with a hidden grin.

John took an interest in teaching me how to stack the oats and rye and meadow grasses. He sent me up on a ladder to the top of the stack where he threw up the bundles. "That's right, Laddie, keep the center of the stack higher than the edges, that's the trick. And be sure to stack the bundles clockwise, as that's the direction that the sun travels. We islanders have tried to stay in tune with nature as best we can for all these years." When I heard his words, I suddenly stopped and gazed off to the blue waters of the Atlantic, slowly repeating "...stay in tune..." over and over again. Down below, John and Kirsti were on their hands and knees gleaning a few loose ends of oats and rye so nothing would go to waste.

Because many of the islanders only spoke Gaelic, I often traveled with a young boy by the name of Ian Paul MacInnes who spoke Gaelic and English. We liked tramping out on the remote eastern shores of the island, across the trackless moors and over the barren hills. Once, while waiting out a particularly violent storm behind a large boulder on the moors, Ian told me how he respected the people out at this end of the island for they were great walkers, strong workers, and hearty individualists. Roads, electricity, and telephones had only been here since the 1970s.

John MacKillob, an old sea captain, lived here in Rhudgarinish.

Captain MacKillob and Ian MacInnes

Eighty-five, he lived alone in a one-room stone cottage on a hillside overlooking the islands of Mull and Skye, lands he had sailed to in wooden boats as a young man. I usually found Captain MacKillob sitting quietly in a blue blazer, soft blue sweater, and pilot's cap at the window seat, looking eastward across the water to the Inner Hebrides. He was always happy to see Ian and me. As soon as we reached his doorway, he was putting water on the stove.

Over tea and sweet biscuits which we had brought from Mary Bremner's store in Loch Carnon, we asked the captain about his days of sailing and fishing the Atlantic waters. He responded generously by taking a tattered shoebox off the shelf that contained photographs of tall ships and tough men, and he told us stories about the storms that took their lives.

The captain often read us some of the poems he had written. He read them slowly in a beautiful thick voice, and he paused once in a while to look up at us. The poems were mostly about a man's love for a woman, perhaps about his departed wife. He poured us glasses of the Grouse between readings and grinned at young Ian Paul as they toasted in Gaelic.

As the afternoon sunlight slid unexpectedly through a small west window and landed gently at our feet, the captain read a few more lines and then stared off to the mountains of Skye. Long still moments of silence crept in, and after a time the captain came back to us, looking into our faces with kind, gentle eyes. "It's been a grand afternoon, lads, and you must come another time." Then he lightly reached out and gave each of our hands a squeeze.

Willie MacPherson was a rugged and handsome-featured fisherman who lived alone in his father's old cottage on the peninsula at Uskivaugh. Willie was nearing sixty and sashayed his strong, muscular body as he walked. He said it was from his many years at sea and from the long walks he took crossing the trackless moors in all kinds of weather for a pint of ale at the Creagorry Inn. Willie was uncle to all the MacInnes children and it was through young Ian Paul that I came to know him.

In late October Willie took Ian and me out on the Atlantic for a full day of lobstering with creels. From dawn to dusk we skirted the banks of the Hebrides in an old wooden boat called the *Golden August*,

throwing out and hauling in close to seventy wooden creels. Enormous quantities of ropes and lines and floats were dispersed without a single tangle or knot.

After a lunch of sandwiches and hot coffee, we rested with the motor shut down, rolling gently on the giant swells that lumbered in off the Atlantic's expanse. Willie stood with young Ian Paul in the stern, his arm around the boy's shoulder, showing him the various components of the engine. They were a handsome sight standing there, with sea birds circling overhead, and the water shimmering like a million diamonds.

When the light off the sea had become flat and made the faces of Willie and the boy seem lined and carved, we made port at Stinky Bay. The day had been memorable but not profitable—only four lobsters from all the traps. Willie, in true Hebridean fashion, handed me the largest lobster as a gift. "Take it, son. You'll enjoy it." Then he turned and made his way through the dusk toward a small fishing cottage at the water's edge.

During my stay with the MacCormicks I often looked out through a small window in the hay loft at a distant cottage on a peninsula called Balagarva. When I asked Angus who lived there, he laughed and said, "It's the old woman who lives in a shoe." A few days later, I went across the low water channel to Balagarva and the small cottage. I knocked on the old door, but no one answered. Then, as I turned to leave, seven of the most beautiful, wide-eyed children emerged from behind the peat pile down by the barn. They stood, motionless as fawns, and stared at me. Their mother appeared from behind the house and introduced herself. "I'm Mary MacInnes. These are the little ones still at home. I had eighteen in all, but most of them have grown up and moved away."

Over tea and scones in Mary MacInnes' tiny kitchen the children, prompted by their mother, shyly introduced themselves. "I'm Dolina." "I'm Moragann." "I'm Archina." "I'm Joan." "I'm Angus John." "I'm Kenny." "I'm Findlay." The father, who had been sleeping under a blanket on the kitchen bed, emerged yawning and stretching. "Hello," he said. "I'm Donald, their Daddy," and he grinned ear to ear.

I promised the children I would bring my tent across to Balagarva

Kenny, Dolina, Findlay, and
Ian MacInnes

Joan, Dolina, and
Moragann MacInnes

16 *Ardnamornie*

Ardnamornie 17

to spend a few nights with them, much to the dismay of the Mac-Cormicks, who thought I would never return. When the children saw me negotiating the stepping stones across the channel, they flew down the embankments and marshy esplanades shrieking, "Wait, Ethan, wait, wait. We'll bring you across horsey-back." The children, though slight of build, were strong and wiry like the fishermen and crofters. Dolina, fourteen, who weighed no more than a hundred pounds, easily carried me across the tidal pools in her bare feet. The little boys, Kenny and Findlay, assured me that horsey-back rides were for everyone; even their father got a ride from their mother when he came home drunk from the dances.

I arrived at their two-room cottage with the children in tow, just as their mother finished darning stockings in the corner by the stove. The children rushed to her, some kneeling at her lap and others trying to whisper in her ear. They spoke to her quietly and with respect, in Gaelic. She nodded her approval and threw me a lovely grin and then went back to her work. The children shrieked and skipped about. "Hide and seek, Ethan. Oh please, please, will you play with us?"

It was a rare and glorious autumn evening. The particles of light in the rain-cleared skies made everything extraordinarily bright and shining. The shore grasses shimmered in luminous greens, the beaches were pure white, and our skin glowed with a rich orange hue, the color of peaches. The children took turns leading me to their favorite hiding places, and it was as though they were showing me their very own hearts. The little boys liked the high knolls of rocks and crags where the woolly sheep slept. The girls preferred the gentleness of the tall, soft grasses that lay between the tidal pools and the marshes.

"Ninety-eight, ninety-nine, one hundred. Ready or not, here I come." Dolina and I lay next to each other, flat on our backs, breathing hard, our hearts racing. We waited, listened, and heard Angus John's footsteps on the ground nearby. Our breathing became slower and rhythmic, became one. The birds were circling overhead, and Gaelic shouts rose in the air. The sea was crashing below us, the marsh grasses bent and swayed above us, and the world seemed round and full, spinning for long minutes without weight or form. Then Angus John crashed through the tall grasses and looked down

Kate Effie MacCormick

Ardnamornie 19

at us like some crofter about to squash a nest of beetles. We made a pathetically funny attempt at running for the goal to save ourselves, but Angus John was like a gazelle, beating us by a hundred strides.

When dusk had covered us, we stumbled home toward a window with a lamp that shone out to the west. Mary had made fresh scones and the little kitchen was warm and smelled of dough baking. She began to feed the children, one at a time. The scones, sweet treacle, and cormorant soup (made from a bird the boys shot on the marsh) seemed like precious gifts to the appreciative children. While some ate, the others went about their evening activities: reading, mending a net, or playing a game of cards with their father on the kitchen bed. And finally, at day's end, the "wireless" played soft Gaelic songs, and the little house became still.

October and November came and went. On my last evening in South Uist, just as we were finishing up dessert at the MacCormicks', a carload of MacInneses in a borrowed taxi appeared in the driveway. They had come to see if anyone was interested in going to the ceilidh at the community hall. Ceilidhs were usual occurances on South Uist, gatherings where people of all ages came together to dance and sing and keep alive the Gaelic traditions. Kate Effie wiped her mouth with her napkin and rose from the table to announce that she was going, and that was that. Her brothers and sisters would have to do the evening chores. I, of course, wasted no time in saying I would accompany her.

Down at the community hall a country orchestra played the tunes of the Hebrides. A crowd had gathered at the gaily decorated tables filled with sandwiches, desserts, hot coffee and tea.

Of all the dances played—jigs, reels, hornpipes, the Gay Gordons—none were livelier, nor more fun to watch than the Boston Quick Step. And of all those who took to the floor, no other couple could compare to Mary and Donald MacInnes. They scooted around the hall in wide circles, arms outstretched, bodies all hunkered down low and fiesty, heads straight ahead as if they were doing the tango.

I asked Kate Effie if she would have a go-round with me on the floor, but she said she would have none of it. Too many tongues were already wagging in the neighborhood from our fish and chips date some weeks back. She was there for the raffle and sat stoically between the minister and old Mary MacDonald, her raffle ticket clasped tightly in her red swollen hands. Dolina MacInnes said she would dance with me, and we made our way to the respective lines of men and women who had assembled for the reel. The men and young boys wore suspenders, woolen pants, and clean white shirts. The women and young girls had long dresses and wore their hair in French braids. As the old-fashioned country orchestra began to play in the simple wooden community hall, a sudden hush fell over the crowd in expectation of the reel. I closed my eyes and felt as if I were in another century.

It was a rainy Sunday morning on my final day in South Uist when I said good-bye to the MacCormicks. The four of them came outside after breakfast and stood silently in front of their home. Kate Effie and Marion were dabbing their eyes with handkerchiefs. Donald and Angus stood limply with their arms at their sides. I shouldered my backpack and went to each of them to exchange a hug. Old Angus trembled and cried and whispered something in Gaelic in my ear as he kissed the side of my head. Gyp, their dog, walked me to the end of their driveway. I turned and waved, and they waved back. For at least twenty minutes, as I headed down the long road to the ferry, we waved at short intervals until we were but mere specks. Then I turned north and looked back no more, bound for the ferry, the mainland, and America.

Old Deschini

TO THE SIERRA MADRE

In early spring of 1981 I traveled down from the snowy mountains of eastern New Mexico in my old VW bus, watching for rabbits on the prairies. I passed through Springer, Solano, Mosquero, Wagon Mound: small prairie towns set in an endless landscape of tall grass and huge skies. The heater was on the fritz, and the sun coming in through the windows barely kept me from freezing. In a small town called Roy, I stopped and rolled out onto the grass, stiff and cold. Roy was one of those *Last Picture Show* towns that dot the American West, a rag-taggle cluster of sagging and forlorn old buildings, silhouetted against a vast sky.

At the Roy Cafe & Pharmacy I warmed myself by a kerosene heater in the back of the building and listened to a group of old railroad men with grimy faces and soft, sad eyes talk about a train wreck down in Tucumcari. When my food arrived, I asked the girl behind the counter—a pretty teenager in blue jeans with a red-checked shirt and a button that pronounced her barrel riding champion for Harding County—if she knew anyone in town who was old-fashioned, someone who still might use draft horses, or knew how to split cedar into fence rails. She said that her grandmother was old-fashioned, that she had been born and bred on the high plains, and that she knew the backcountry as well as anyone in these parts. We talked for a while, and when I paid the check she drew a map on a napkin, showing me where I could find her grandmother. It was just two blocks down the street. She smiled and wished me luck.

I found the old grandmother sitting out of the wind in a straight-backed chair that caught the sunlight on the south side of the house. She spoke no English, but welcomed me in Spanish. I responded in my high school Spanish, introduced myself, and explained that I was traveling around the country talking with people about the land and local history. She smiled, motioned for me to sit down and for nearly an hour, as the sun warmed us, she slowly and passionately talked about her life.

Her name was Luisa Lucero and she was a prairie midwife and herb gatherer, *una partera*, as she liked to call herself. For almost fifty years—between droughts, dust bowls, depressions, and world wars—she had practiced midwifery, traveling alone by horseback and wagon to the ranches and homesteads spread across these high plains.

When her husband died, and the buildings of their old ranch fell into disrepair, Luisa moved into town. She lived with her grand-daughter's family in a modern house on a residential street in Roy, and spent much of her time in an over-stuffed chair beside the television, which was left on all day. Luisa said she pretended to watch it to please her family, but when the granddaughter did laundry, she would sneak out the back door and go to the edge of the prairie. There, unencumbered and alone, she would wander in freedom and solitude.

At eighty-three Luisa still gathered the roots and plants that grew on the prairie. She knew them as others might know common phar-maceutical products. Immortal root and malva plant were her two favorites, her best "allies," as she liked to call them. She kept stashes of them in an old gunnysack underneath her bed. Each season old friends would stop by for some of Luisa's remedies.

On two occasions I went to visit Luisa Lucero and the family allowed us to gather medicinal plants. We walked easily with one another, like children, bending and stooping to inspect a plant or a root, gazing skyward to watch a hawk or an eagle making concentric circles in the sky. She was a strong woman, spare and wiry, with the gait of a woman half her age.

Sometimes Luisa wandered away from me to sit alone on a hillock to the east. There, she let the wind come full into her face, and her long white hair blew in wisps about her head. She later told me she was remembering when she had been a practicing midwife on these prairies, picturing in her mind the way it had been. One night her cabin door had suddenly swung open and a dark-skinned boy with anxious eyes stood there breathing hard. He told her that it was time

Luisa Lucero

Des-Bah-Bay-Ah grinding corn,
Canyon de Chelly

and asked if she would come and help with the birthing. Telling her husband not to worry, she dressed hurriedly, followed the boy to his horse, mounted her own, and rode off to a distant light in the mountains where a rancher's family listened for the sound of the horses' return. She had delivered three hundred babies on these plains: three hundred rides deep into the hills.

A few days later I found myself heading west, traveling back roads to northern Arizona to help some Navajo friends with their spring planting of corn. Fred and Mary Tayah were old friends of mine. We had stayed in touch over the years by mail, and once or twice a year I would show up unexpectedly at their cabin—"Indian time" (whenever you get there). They were herders who had been born down in Canyon de Chelly. Now nearing sixty, they lived in a small cabin on the south rim of the canyon. They planted a big garden, chopped wood, hauled rain water from seep holes in the cliffs, and lived without the use of an automobile, telephone, or electricity. I liked spending time with them; the beauty and solitude of their old cabin on the mesa brought me peace and joy. They called me their "little boy" and gave me the Navajo name of Bahozoni, which means "everything good in front of you."

When not herding sheep, Fred and Mary often took me down into the canyon on old Anasazi trails. They knew the canyon's fifty-mile labyrinth of mazes, and Mary's old mother, a spare, resolute herder of eighty-three by the name of Des-Bah-Bay-Ah, still lived there in a simple wooden hogan. I loved visiting with the old woman. She made us Navajo fried bread and heated goat's milk over a small outdoor fire. We sat by the river to eat and watched Indian boys riding fast horses north to the mountains. At dusk, when the canyon was bathed in an orange light, Des-Bah-Bay-Ah trailed her sheep and goats along the ancient pathways, her Navajo herding songs echoing off the red rock walls and floating up out of the canyon.

Fred and Mary did not have a car or pick-up, so I would take them down to Chinle to do their shopping at Garcia's Trading Post. I loved to see the Navajos leaning up against the building warming their bodies in the morning sunlight. One old man, a tall willowy herder with deep-set blue eyes and a slouched herder's hat, caught my eye. When I asked Fred and Mary who he was, they told me his name was Old Deschini. He lived with his wife's family in Many Farms, a desert Indian village bordered by the mountains. During the day he was a

Mrs. Deschini

Old Deschini

farmer, working his fields into long rows of corn, beans, and squash. At night he was the community's medicine man, walking long miles through the barren hills to help heal friends and neighbors. His teachings were thousands of years old: songs and dances, prayers and chants, medicinal plants and potions. He carried a leather pouch at his waist containing bones, feathers, and claws. Old Deschini's father had also been a medicine man.

The first time Fred and Mary introduced me to Old Deschini, he was leaving to start a three-day vision quest. He headed off on foot, looking like an old coyote as he walked through the desert from Garcia's Trading Post toward a nearby mountain top. Fred, at my prompting, asked him to come for supper when he came down off the mountain. The old man smiled and said that he would be happy to, but only if they served him mutton.

Days later Old Deschini appeared at Fred and Mary's doorway just as Mary was getting food on the table for supper. The old man took off his hat and coat, made talk with Fred for a few minutes, and then sat down at the table and waited for his meal in silence. When it arrived, he seized the plate with both hands and drew it close to him, his long, slender fingers picking up the juicy meat and sucking on the bones and gristle. No talk, no eye contact, just an old Navajo with his mutton. When he had finished, he pushed his plate away and slowly looked up and smiled, his blue eyes radiating an appreciation that went beyond words.

I soon began spending time with Old Deschini at his small farm in the desert. I enjoyed coming in the late afternoon when the desert shadows were long and purple. Often Mrs. Deschini, a tall, lithe woman with a beatific smile, wove on her loom in the dooryard. A grandchild sat beside her, watching her create the designs of her tribe. Old Deschini came home from the fields with a hoe and a shovel over his shoulder, and he rested underneath the cottonwood trees as a grandchild brought him his supper on a tin plate.

Old Deschini was fascinating to be around: tall, silent, and mystical. He had the most amazing eyes I have ever seen, luminous pools of turquoise, and his hands were large and smooth as a snake's skin. He did not speak English and I did not speak Navajo, but we got on well together. He sensed I wished to learn about the desert, the canyon, and the history of his people.

One afternoon he took me down into the canyon on steep, treacherous trails where cedar ladders spanned great chasms, and where the finger holds in the cliffs were no bigger than buttons. When we came to the valley floor, we followed a clear stream north to the Lukachukai Mountains. Soon we passed a side canyon with red rock walls a thousand feet high. By late afternoon, with the sun reflecting off the canyon walls, the sand here was hot to the touch. Old Deschini told me it was good for taking sickness and fatigue from the body.

At his prompting I removed my clothes and put them in a pile at the base of a juniper tree. The old man walked around in a circle for a minute or two—like an old brown lizard about to burrow in the sand—and then pointed to a spot where he instructed me to lie down. Then he left me, walking down the canyon the way we had come. I scooped up handfuls of the hot sand and covered my entire body, leaving only my head free. Something in my body immediately let go. It was as if my backbone had suddenly snapped, and I was melting down into the warm earth. I drifted in and out of consciousness and listened to the trickle of the stream a few yards away and to the sound of a warbler in a nearby bush. When I awoke, perhaps an hour later, the stiffness and weariness had disappeared from my body, and I lay up against the base of a tree watching white clouds in the sky forming and reforming in the early evening.

A few days later I said good-bye to Fred and Mary and traveled to the Papago Indian Reservation in southern Arizona. There I met two old Papagos—a brother and a sister—living in an adobe compound in the Sonoran Desert. They were old Indians, born near the turn of the century in a cave in the mountains. Their grandmother had assisted in their birthing, and when the children were old enough to walk, the old woman led her family out into the desert to live as traditional nomads. She taught them how to find water in the ground, how to make fire from greasewood sticks, and how to gather the sweet sticky fruit from the saguaro cactus.

Now, seventy years later, the brother and sister were living together outside a small Indian town called Topawa. They were generous and offered me a grass-and-driftwood *ramada* (lean-to) to sleep under. At night the skies were alive with sharp-pointed stars. Sometimes near daybreak I heard the coyotes howling—an electric,

Laura praying at dawn

ethereal singing—and I was never sure whether I had imagined the sound, or if they really gathered there on the other side of the hill. When dawn came, a soft yellow light eased out onto the desert, and I heard the brother and sister stirring in their quarters. Soon afterward they made their way along a worn path to a simple wooden altar. There, with the first light falling upon them, they began their day with Papago songs and prayers that floated out over the pink-tinged sands like whispers.

The brother's name was Hoosie. He reminded me of Ishi, the last aboriginal Indian who walked out of the mountains of northern California to surrender to the modern world. Hoosie was silent and secretive, and while I spent almost eight days near him, I cannot say I ever came to understand him. He spoke no English and rarely, if ever, ventured outside his desert compound. He lived in an old chicken coop beside the main adobe and took all his meals there alone. His life was his garden; he was masterful with things that grew. While crops of beans, melons, and corn prospered, he prized most his long beds of wheat. When it was too hot to work, Hoosie would sit in the shade and grind wheat berries on an old stone grinder that had once belonged to his grandmother.

Sometimes when I went to town—a place that Hoosie never went—I returned with a small gift for him. Once I brought him a jar of cold, sweet grape juice. He took the jar in the searing noon heat, gulped it down in six swallows, and as the juice dribbled down his chin, he stared at me with wonder in his dark eyes. Another time I brought him a bundle of rawhide leather strips from a cobbler in Tucson. He held them in his large hands for a long time, muttering low, deep sounds as he fondled the smooth leather. Sometimes Hoosie brought me things: a snake's skull, a raven's feather, a ripe melon. He stood close to me and handled the object awkwardly, speaking softly and shyly in Papago, and when he thought it was the right time, he pushed the gift toward me and then turned and made his way back to his gardening.

His sister Laura was gregarious and spoke English perfectly. She was a fine potter and worked at her kiln every day, fashioning beautiful vessels from the red clay that she found along the dry river beds. A modern Indian in many ways, she once flew with her church group to Assisi in Italy to pay homage to her beloved Saint Francis.

But underneath the modern veneer ran the blood of a desert nomad. Once, when I knocked over a glass of water at dinner, she made a horrible, sickening sound as the liquid ran off the table and was swallowed by the desert. Later she apologized to me for her reaction, telling me that she had never become accustomed to an abundance of water.

Occasionally in the late afternoon Laura and Hoosie took me deep into the desert on worn Indian trails to a saguaro cactus. Laura took delight in teaching me how to use wooden pincers to remove the fruit from the spiny cactus. She told me her grandmother had taken them to this same cactus when they were children.

In the evening, after Hoosie was fed and retired for the night, Laura and I ate outside by candlelight at an old wooden table beside her kiln. It was a beautiful time of day: the lingering heat from the desert clung to our skin and the fragrance of the flowers in the garden Laura lovingly tended surrounded us. She cooked in the morning, so I cooked our evening meal. When it was ready, I called her and she appeared in the doorway looking like a young schoolgirl, with her hair done up in ribbons, wearing a beautiful blouse and skirt. I escorted her to the table where our dinner waited in earthen bowls Laura had made: salad, rice, guacamole, red peppers, tomatoes, dark bread, and a chilled bottle of wine. We reached across the table and took each other's hands for the blessing, soft words in English and Papago, prayers for friends and family, for Mother Earth and Grandfather Sky.

In early April, when the desert was in bloom, I left Laura and Hoosie and crossed into Mexico on a dusty back road. The border crossing was a solitary desert outpost where a Mexican custom agent in an ill-fitting suit took a long time going through my van. When he came to my stash of bee pollen, ginseng, and wheat germ I froze in terror, but he was a country man and recognized them when I explained in delinquent Spanish. He waved me on and wished me well, making a low sweeping bow and doffing his cap as I drove into the morning of a Mexican spring day.

The great Sonoran Desert stretched out in all directions. Mountain range after mountain range sloped to the south where back roads suddenly disappeared, ravaged by flash floods. Near sunset, on the highway somewhere between Caborea and Magdalena, I pulled off the road, grabbed a bedroll and a knapsack, and walked out into the desert

as far as I dared. The sand was rippled where the wind had passed earlier in the day, and the delicate smell of juniper hovered above the earth. I stopped and built a small fire, brewed tea, and stretched out on the still-warm sand. Two stars appeared in the east and the new moon hung softly on a crag in the nearby mountains.

Days later, traveling south along the Sonora River Valley, I came upon a small farming community called Arizpe. Arizpe was a traditional village with twisting narrow streets of white-washed adobes. The church, made of cut white stone, had been built in 1654. During the day men and women came through town with horses and burros loaded with corn, beans, garlic, onions, seeds, and nuts for the market. Children played on flat stones in the plaza. Old campesinos in shredded huarache sandals and white pants sat on the church steps warming their stooped shoulders in the early spring sunshine.

I lived by the Sonora River for more than a week, camping beside it, walking its banks every day, and visiting the local families who worked small *milpas* (farms) growing corn and beans. They were friendly country people. Most of them had never seen a *norteamericano* before, let alone spoken to one. I saw them down by the river in the cottonwood trees with their sheep and cattle, whispering in small groups as they watched me. I tried to keep a pot of coffee on my campfire during the day, and when I beckoned to them, they came up in groups of two and three and sat cross-legged on the earth by the fire. We spoke in Spanish, drank cups of strong coffee, and ate handfuls of trail mix from a wooden bowl. They were good honest people who liked to laugh and joke.

A frequent visitor to my campsite was a one-legged nut gatherer by the name of Socorro Gonzales. Socorro, seventy, lived upriver in a small cabin with his wife. She kept the chickens, did their laundry on the flat rocks by the river, and swore at the burros when they got into the corn. Socorro was a blacksmith by profession. He made strong stirrups and saddle horns for his neighbors from ore that he found in the mountains. It was from nut gathering, however, that he made his living. Two or three times a week he would pass my camp on his burro, with sacks of shelled pecans hanging from the saddle. He was kind and often took me with him into the mountains to gather nuts. I watched, amazed, as he pulled himself from the saddle into the trees, climbing high into the limbs. He looked like a young schoolboy as he gathered

the pecans into gunnysacks. When the sacks were full, and the shadows grew long and purple, Socorro took me home for a hot supper of black beans, tortillas, and dried strips of beef. With his wife we sat together on the ground by the fire, drinking coffee, and sharing stories as the stars came out over the mountains.

Wherever I traveled in Mexico—from Sonora to Sinaloa—I was always treated well. One night while driving on a back road in the logging country of southern Chihuahua, my VW bus went off the road and hung precariously over a cliff. I yelled in bad Spanish for help, and a grandfather and two boys came running through the dusk. They managed to pull me back onto the road. The old man, Isodoro Rascon, was a gangly farmer with missing teeth and a thin face. He invited me home for supper and to spend the night. His wife, Palma, served a meal of rice, beans, and fresh tortillas as I warmed myself by the fire.

It felt good to be out of the cold. Isodoro and Palma lived in a pine forest in the mountains, sharing a one-room cabin with their two small granddaughters, Rosa and Ramona. We gathered around the fire after supper to talk, mostly about their crops and animals, but also about my home in the United States. I brought out small gifts for the family: for the grownups there were small bottles of Harvey's Bristol Cream Sherry (which they sampled with tablespoons), and for the children a bag of sweets (from Mrs. Gooch's Natural Food Store in Los Angeles)—dried pineapple rings, carob-coated peanuts, and long thin sticks of black licorice.

When the chickens came inside the house to roost, the old couple led me down through the pasture to a stream where stars and the new moon were reflected in black icy pools. Then we went up past a sickle of lingering snow to a pine barn where they kept corn. As Palma held the lantern, Isodoro gathered up armfuls of corn stalks and made a bed on the floor. He patted it with his hand and assured me that I would sleep well there. Before they left, with the light from the lantern shining on their faces, they each took one of my hands and told me how honored they felt to have me spend the night with them.

In the morning I said good-bye to Isodoro and Palma, kissed the little girls, and continued on some forty miles south to a town called Creel. The mountains were shrouded in rain and fog, and the road was swallowed up in places where swift-flowing rivers crossed it. I had to make running starts with the van to forge these rivers: great arcs of water shot out from each tire, and rocks nearly up-ended me. It was scary business for a non-mechanic like myself (who *did* know rivers could stall an engine). But the gods of the Volkswagens were with me and I made it safely through all the river crossings, reaching the town of Creel at dusk, as lights began to appear on the hillsides.

Creel was a logging town in the high Sierra Tarahumara of southern Chihuahua. Old logging trucks ground their way up and down the dusty main street. Mexican farmers came through town with horses and burros loaded with produce. The sweet smell of pinyon smoke drifted in the air, rising from the chimneys of a group of log shacks. I spent the first night at a railroad hostelry where itinerant Mexicans slept: dormitory-like rooms with a porcelain wash basin and pitcher, a simple kerosene lamp, and an outdoor privy. At night, as cold descended into the valley, families cooked delicious-smelling meals in their rooms, babies laughed, old men told jokes, and teenage boys strummed guitars and sang haunting love songs. A dollar a night bought an ambience far more welcoming than any I have found in a Holiday Inn.

I had come to Creel to see the Tarahumara Indians, who lived in caves and stone huts in the high back country. Perhaps the most traditional indigenous group of native Americans between the Arctic Circle and the Amazon, they were a large group—forty thousand or more—who lived on one of the most demanding landscapes of the North American continent. They worked tiny plots of stony land, growing their corn and beans at staggering elevations—twelve and thirteen thousand feet. In contrast, they herded their sheep at the bottom of Barranca de Cobre, the deepest canyon in the world. They ate rattlesnakes and wolves, eels and lizards, roots and berries, and rarely, if ever, descended into the villages of the white man's world. The Mexicans called them *cimarones* (the wild ones). The white man called them Tarahumaras. But they preferred to call themselves *raramuri* (the runners).

Almost all of the Tarahumaras could run long distances—twenty, fifty, one hundred, two hundred miles—on a bellyful of corn and a flask of peyote juice, while kicking a small wooden ball for sport. When the governor of Mexico requested that they send runners to the 1920

Sebastian

track and field events in Mexico City, the Tarahumaras sent down two young girls. They understood that the race was to be no longer than twenty-six miles.

There was a settlement of Tarahumaras living in San Ignacio, a small hamlet of stone houses and log cabins. I spent a week there, sleeping and cooking in my van, tramping through the hills, and exploring the canyons and mountainsides. Wherever I hiked I would see them: shepherds in white tunics with red sashes about their heads and waists, women in calico skirts and white blouses collecting firewood on the flanks of the mountains. They were shy and cautious, and would disappear when they caught sight of me. They vanished down side canyons into the folds of boulders, sprang up cliffs where they were swallowed by the thick forest. Elusive and solitary, they reminded me of deer that had been hunted to near extinction.

While living in the mission at San Ignacio, I got to know one of the Tarahumaras, a retired mail carrier who lived in a cave in the mountains. I met Sebastian Venturia, a short stocky Indian nearing seventy, one afternoon while tramping through the hills above the mission, and he welcomed me in Spanish and gestured for me to come in and visit.

I made a number of calls on Sebastian, sometimes during the day when the barefoot old man trailed his herds of sheep and goats out into the plain, but more often at night, when he was sure to be home. I loved to walk up from the valley into the hills. The old, worn pathways held a magical fascination for me, twisting their circuitous routes through the boulder-strewn ravines. Sebastian usually sat by a fire at the entrance to his cave, weaving large rugs and blankets. It was a good place to sit and listen to the old man. The sheep and goats were asleep in a corner on the sandy floor, hens and roosters gathered in the other corner on small tree-like perches. The cave seemed to pulsate eerily as the whitewashed walls caught the firelight. I enjoyed listening to Sebastian telling tales of his years as a mailman and courier in the high Sierras. He once ran a distance of nearly six hundred miles in just under nine days. Of all the things the old man discussed, I especially enjoyed hearing about the peyote celebrations in distant stone villages, and about the races where Tarahumaras ran one hundred miles or more in a single day.

During my first few days with the Tarahumaras I was surprised to find that no one came out to visit me even though there was a steady

flow of shepherds and farmers on the plain. One evening, while cooking rice and beans in my van, a crowd of Tarahumara children appeared at the back of the car. They stood silent and motionless staring at me. I smiled at them, welcomed them in Spanish, and gestured for them to come see the interior of the van. I could see that they were shy and afraid—they stood their ground. I smiled and continued with my cooking, and then it occured to me that perhaps they would like a picture of themselves. Rummaging for my Polaroid I found it and snapped a picture of the group. I handed the print to the tallest girl, a pretty teenager with long braids and a beautiful woven shawl about her shoulders. I watched as a smile came onto her face. She whispered to the others, who gathered around her to watch the images appearing. They became excited and animated, and several of the smaller children lost their fear and came to ask me for a portrait of themselves. Then, for nearly an hour, the sun high enough in the sky to illuminate their beautiful faces, I made individual portraits of all twenty-five children. When I was finished, I gave them a tour of the van, complete with a look at a scrapbook of my own family, home, and village back in New England. When they left, each child walked away slowly with a picture clasped close to her chest.

I decided to make the long drive through Central Mexico to see my mother, who was vacationing in the mountain town of San Miguel de Allende. The last I had heard from her was in a letter I received while in Arizona. She was staying at a small, elegant hotel. She wrote that she was getting good exercise by walking the streets and hillsides around the town and that she had met a handful of interesting American women. A postscript mentioned how much she loved Mexico and the local people. The drive down and back would add an additional fifteen hundred miles to my trip, but I wanted to see her.

My mother thought I was in Arizona with my Indian friends, so I decided to surprise her. I spotted her on my second morning in San Miguel de Allende—white-haired, kind-faced, browsing in the marketplace with a friend—and watched her from behind some bushes in the central plaza for nearly fifteen minutes. It seemed extraordinary to observe my mother here, far from home, completely out of context. As she drew closer, I jumped out of the bushes and gave her a big hug. She nearly had a heart attack and stood there with a numbed expres-

sion on her face, trying to figure out whether I was an apparition or the real thing. Finally we sat down on a park bench and rested, gathered in our emotions, and regained a somewhat normal composure. Then we laughed, hard and long. She told me that just a half hour before she had seen a barefoot traveler in blue jeans, hair flying all over the place, crossing the park. She had jokingly remarked to her companion, "Look at that traveler, Helen. You know, I've got a freak for a son who could pass as his double."

For a week my mother and I spent time together in beautiful San Miguel: we took morning coffee and afternoon tea on the terraces and walked on narrow cobblestone streets searching for rugs and small gifts to bring home. Sometimes we just sat on a tree-lined avenue watching women doing their outdoor laundry on flat stones. Once we took a drive to a nearby village and walked up into the mountains on a herders' path and enjoyed the long views to the south. An occasional child stopped and made conversation with us. At night I showered and shaved in a fountain in the rear of a park (when no one was looking), rummaged in the back of my van for a coat and tie and clean white shirt, and appeared at eight o'clock for the formal meal at the Hotel del Bosque, where my mother was staying.

Of all the sights in San Miguel—churches, plazas, old villas, Indians selling weavings on the street, the local people taking the night air in the park—the one that touched us the most was an old Mexican couple in their eighties who shuffled through the streets holding onto each other. They were a sad and yet an inspirational sight, old people at the very end of their lives. Though not beggars in the true sense, they did accept money from passersby. Their names were Martín and Zoamilla Silva, and they lived on the outskirts of San Miguel. According to a local merchant, they had been married for fifty-seven years.

One afternoon, as we watched the Silvas struggling in the heat and traffic, my mother suggested that I offer them a ride home in my van. When I asked if they would care for a ride, they graciously accepted. Driving south out of town, I asked them where their house was. "Adelante, adelante," they said and pointed with gnarled old hands to a forlorn-looking hillside.

We parked and walked along debris-strewn pathways that wound in and around the village dump. Nearing a grove of giant cottonwood trees, the Silvas came to a shuffling halt. When I asked them where

Martín and Zoamilla Silva

their house was, they pointed to the base of the trees. All I could see was a charred fire pit, a tarp, a box of clothing, an over-stuffed red chair with a spring hanging out, and some pots and pans. When I asked them again where their house was they simply said, "La tierra esta nuestra casa (the earth is our home)." Martín and Zoamilla Silva lived on the ground.

In the morning my mother gave me some money to take to the Silvas. They wished me well on my journey home. Soon after, I packed up my van, had a final shave in the fountain, and had breakfast with my mother on the terrace of the Hotel del Bosque. Our paths had crossed and now we were parting, she for Mexico City and her flight home, me for a long, long drive north—bound for a small New England village of white clapboard houses and neat picket fences, a place I often call home.

Down the valley for
winter provisions

THE MANANG TREK

In October of 1982 I traveled to Nepal, hoping to live in the mountain villages of the Himalayas. Nepal had intrigued me ever since I first heard of its towering mountains, raging rivers, and indomitable people. In many ways Nepal seemed an anachronism: a medieval nation of thirteen million people in a modern world. It stretched six hundred miles without roads, electricity, or modern communications. Even when wandering the back streets of the capital, Kathmandu, I felt as if I were thrown back in time a thousand years.

When I arrived, I learned that a friend from Vermont was living in the Kathmandu valley. Sahra Aschenbach and I had spent time together in Burlington, where she had been a holistic health practitioner and therapist. The last I had heard of her was in a newspaper clipping that showed her selling everything she owned at a yard sale in order to raise money to go to Asia. Two years later Sahra was living in a small farming village called Swayambu, sharing a house with a Dutch traveler named Mariel, and studying Tibetan Buddhism at a nearby monastery.

I stayed with Sahra and Mariel for several weeks as I made preparations for a trek in the mountains. Their three-story brick house had large, open rooms with windows that looked out to a white Buddhist temple on a distant hill. Below the house there were green terraced fields of ripe barley and rice where villagers in traditional dress labored. An old path that wound from the lowlands of Kathmandu to the mountains of Pokhara passed by the house. Everything and everyone rode upon the path: gaggles of geese, tall white goats, laughing children, turbaned elders, and men carrying sheaves of grain. Twenty-five hundred years ago, another traveler walked this

very path, a man named Shakyamuni Buddha.

We often rose before the first light in the morning and sat up on our roof in sleeping bags watching a torch-lit procession of villagers bringing their market produce in from the outlying districts. They carried flaming branches to light their way along the path, and their hushed voices floated up to us in the thick fog. From our perches high above the trail, these long illuminated lines of floating hayricks seemed ghostly, like foxfire etchings on a Chinese scroll.

During the day we often went into Kathmandu together. It was a beautiful walk that took us through forests and glades, along rivers, over bridges, past markets, and along cobblestone streets. Kathmandu was like no other city I had ever seen. On any street corner you might find yourself surrounded by holy men in loin cloths, businessmen in three-piece suits, hippies from Freak Street, Tibetans, Sikhs, or even a huge white bull.

We enjoyed spending our evenings together on the roof, where we danced to music while we cooked dinner on a small Primus stove. Thousands of bats, as large as cats, flew home to the mountains at this hour. We used to lie in our sleeping bags and watch them as they flew overhead. Down to the west, the lights of Swayambu Temple shimmered in the dusk. The devotional music of the Tibetan households above us on the hillside spilled into the valley like rippling water.

For three weeks Sahra's house in Swayambu was my home, and then it was time to go. My dream of trekking over the Thorong La Pass became more pressing because by December snow would block the route. Each morning I could see fresh snow on the distant peaks, and in the early morning I often found a thin shell of ice on the puddles in the garden.

In early November, while looking at trekking equipment in a mountaineering shop in Kathmandu, the young Tibetan proprietress introduced me to a Sherpa man who said he was familiar with the route and would be happy to serve as my guide. His name was Kipa and he was a Sherpa from the Solo Khumbu region in eastern Nepal. With the help of the shopkeeper, who spoke both English and Nepalese, Kipa and I were able to make plans and preparations for a mid-November start.

Kipa was a delight to be around; he was gentle, easygoing, and had a good sense of humor. He spoke no English, and I, no Nepalese, but we somehow managed to communicate effectively with each other along the trail—mostly through pantomimes that often made us laugh. He looked after me untiringly—cooking, setting up camp, making sure I did not drink from fouled streams, or sleep where it was dangerous. He also intuitively knew the kind of people I wanted to see—old hermits, friendly grandmothers, and vagabonds. He had an inexhaustible supply of them and was forever bringing me to old friends along the route who seemed happy to let us sleep in their barn or house in exchange for some work or a gift of food.

Kipa also helped me take pictures, even though I suspected he had never handled a camera before. We practiced on village children. I showed him how to focus the camera and pleaded with him not to chop off people's heads or feet. Kipa would laugh, and I did not know until I got home whether the five hundred pictures he had taken were any good. (They were.)

We walked slowly through the mountains, taking time when the spirit moved us to work with the villagers harvesting grain and rice. In a mountain village called Bahundanda we spent two days helping a family cut and bind their barley. I am not sure whether I was a help or a hindrance, as the oxen and the bison were spooked by my smell, and the young women spent more time twittering and staring at me than they did at their own work.

In a tiny village called Tal, on the far side of the Annapurnas, we spent the night with one of the many *ammas* (mothers) that Kipa knew along the way. As I wandered through the village, I met a Tibetan-looking man resting on a stone bench in the late afternoon sunshine. I motioned to ask if I might join him and he gestured for me to sit down. "Are you Tibetan?" I asked him. "No," he replied, "Larki man." He threw a gnarled old hand eastward toward a waterfall on a distant mountain and then held up four fingers and did a funny little walk with them to tell me that it was a four day walk to his Larki village. He wore his hair in two long braids bound together with strips of red cloth. His cloak and ripped leggings smelled of damp wool and rancid grease. On his feet he wore yakskin boots. He eyed my camera on the bench between us, picked it up correctly, and aimed it at the surrounding peaks, muttering faint ahhhs and mmms all the while. When he laid it back down, he did a pantomime with his twitching fingers and

Cattle threshing grain

Upper Pisang (11,000 feet)

expressive eyes that told me he enjoyed the way the telephoto lens made distant things look close.

I treated the two of us to tea and biscuits and brought out a packet of assorted needles. I motioned that he could choose six. He painstakingly went over every needle for several minutes and then decided upon six. These he carefully transferred to a worn leather sewing kit he carried on a sash around his waist. He patted his sewing kit three times and grinned at me.

In the remote mountain villages tourists were a rarity. In one village Kipa and I were followed through the streets by a group of nearly fifty people; many believed I was a doctor dispensing medical supplies. One old man in a white tunic burst through the crowd to show me a gaping head wound he had received a week before. It was a nasty cut, deep and infected, with dirt and hay chaff caught in the dried blood. Kipa and I washed and dressed the wound, and showed him how to do it himself with the supplies we gave him. The villagers watched me intently. I felt as though I were Albert Schweitzer.

Two long weeks trekking on the winding mountain trails brought us to the fringe of the high Tibetan Plateau and our first Buddhist village, Pisang. Encircled by the looming peaks of the Annapurna, Lamjung, and Manaslu mountains, the village sat in a crystalline arctic desert at close to eleven thousand feet. It was a village with about fifty families living in a single stone and timber complex, much like the pueblo villages of the Hopi and Zuñi in the American Southwest.

We arrived in Pisang in the late afternoon as the towering peaks eclipsed the winter sun. Villagers were returning from the fields, dark-skinned Tibetans in long robes carrying plows on their backs and leading oxen. Kipa recognized an old couple who seemed over-joyed to see him. While they talked, I lingered by a gray river, watching golden eagles soaring in the dull skies overhead, and listened to rooftop prayer flags snapping in the piercing wind.

Soon Kipa returned and took me to the home where we were to spend the night. We entered through a stone stable that housed a woolly bull calf and a black nanny goat and then made our way along a dark corridor to the main living space. The dark and smoky room was illuminated by two candles and several fireplaces. When my eyes became accustomed to the low light, I was welcomed by the family who stood waiting to be introduced. The father and mother, old uncle, grandmother and grandfather, and handful of smudgy-faced children in long pigtails were recent refugees from Tibet.

The father and the old uncle sat cross-legged on the hearth spinning prayer wheels in one hand and counting wooden prayer beads in the other. Above them on the mantel was the family altar with burning candles, a wooden Buddha, and a picture of the Dalai Lama. Nearby on the earthen floor the old grandmother and grandfather sat sorting out dried grains that would later be ground into flour. The mother tended a hundred things at once: she churned salt tea, stirred *tukpa* (noodle stew) and checked the fermenting *chiang* (beer) all while nursing an infant with a wonderfully round bottom. From time to time she called across the room to the children, who were tending a caldron of stewing meat on the small fire.

The old grandmother served me my dinner by the fire: stew with yak meat, Tibetan bread, and strong salt tea with rancid yak butter. Every time I took a sip, she seemed to be at my side to refill my cup. The night wind moaning about the eaves seemed portentous. Five men suddenly staggered through the small doorway, looking like apparitions from an ancient hunt. They stood motionless in their hides until the *amma* motioned for them draw near the fire. There they hunkered down on squat legs and warmed their outstretched hands. I sat nearby and slowly searched their lined faces. They were Tibetans too, old hunters with squinty eyes and wispy black mustaches and chin hairs. The father and uncle seemed happy they had come, and they soon began telling jokes and high-spirited stories, filling the room with their entertainment. They were carefree, spontaneous guests, whose laughter shook their limbs from ears to toes.

When the hunters left, and the hearth fires had died down to red coals, I lay on sheep skins the old grandfather had brought me. The father and old uncle resumed their chanting, and the mother lay in a pile of blankets on the floor with her children. Kipa was on the hearth braiding horsehair into rope for a present to give to the family. I drifted in and out of sleep. At some point during the night, I remembered Kipa coming to drape a wool blanket over me, touching my shoulder with his hand and saying something in Nepalese as he blew out the candle.

Entering the Manang Valley (12,000 feet)

We left the Tibetan family in the morning after a breakfast of roasted barley and fresh yak milk. We climbed higher and higher into the Tibetan Plateau, passing from one valley into another. A few days later we arrived at a town called Manang, a few acres that sat precariously at twelve thousand feet. It was a Buddhist village, close to the Tibetan border, with shrieking winds and a cold sandy soil that begrudgingly yielded a meager harvest of potatoes and grain. I was wearing all the clothes I had and I was still cold. Solid ice filled the horse troughs at the edge of the village. Hunters with deep, searching eyes were leaving for the mountains as we arrived. Manang, a village of cold and scarcities, was nine days in either direction from the nearest road. The winter before, when food supplies had dwindled, a party of toughened men set out over the pass to Tibet and returned with thirty yaks which they slaughtered for the village.

In Manang we stayed on a rooftop that belonged to an old woman Kipa knew. She appreciated guests, and allowed us to chop her wood and haul her water. She also let us cook for her, meals she normally would not have prepared for herself: pancakes with honey-lemon syrup, cheese omelettes, and a sweet pudding made from yak's milk.

In the late afternoon of our first day in Manang a band of teenagers began singing and dancing on rooftops throughout the village. It was the beginning of the Tibetan New Year, and the villagers celebrated it with a fierce passion. Blood-curdling screams and hard-driving drum beats pierced the heart of this mountain town. Though I had never heard Tibetan music before, the songs were distinctly familiar, very much like those of the Navajo, Apache, and Sioux.

By dusk the night revelers had come to a rooftop that abutted ours, and with a precarious leap of five feet or more I drew close to the throng, now gyrating and pulsing like a Chinese dragon. About ten young men danced clockwise with ten young women. There were two male drummers who wailed as they beat huge yakskin drums in the center of the circle. Their long black hair fell loosely and caught bits of firelight from the kitchen fires. The circling crowd moved hypnotically with small, rhythmic steps. They looked like North American Indians but moved with slightly oriental gestures and had upturned, slender fingers. I drew as close as I dared without attracting attention. Their garments brushed my fingertips, and the smells of yak wool and wood smoke flew about my face and made me giddy. I

Muktinath, below Thorong La Pass

was only a few inches from squeezing into the circle for a midnight go-round, but a hand on my shoulder stopped me, and I turned to find Kipa. The *amma* wanted us to come for dinner.

Several days later and many long miles farther into the plateau, Kipa and I camped at fourteen thousand feet at the base of the Thorong La Pass. In the bitter cold of early morning Kipa rapped gently on the tent flaps. He had brought hot tea and the news that a fire had been made. I lingered in my sleeping bag with ponderous thoughts of the day to come. Yesterday's long haul on the trail had been cold and difficult for me (I found the high altitudes punishing) and I had spent a miserable night, most of the time at the bottom of the sleeping bag looking for a warm spot that was not there.

Dawn broke clear and cold, and the first light of the sun spilled thinly onto the massive peak of Niligiri. It was bitter cold in the ravine—five below or less—and we huddled around Kipa's small fire trying to ease the cold from our bones.

We ate breakfast hurriedly. The wind had not yet come up, and we were anxious to take advantage of the gift. Climbing up toward fifteen thousand feet required all the energy I could muster. My breathing was labored and pained, and my legs and back ached. I had to rest every ten or fifteen steps. Kipa was at my side the whole time, encouraging me with soft words.

By midmorning we had cleared the rock-strewn lower section of the mountain and had emerged at the edge of a vast white kingdom of snowfields and looming peaks. We could count sixteen mountains of twenty thousand feet or more. Now, for some reason, the trek up the newly fallen snow seemed easier. Perhaps it was the light, or the poorly defined trail, but I became somewhat delirious. At these high altitudes everyday thoughts seemed to vanish. Instead I thought only of the moment—my boots crunching on the snow, the wind tearing at my face, the weight of the pack, my straining lungs, the depth of the blue sky, the sparkling snow.

By midday we had come to almost eighteen thousand feet and the final five hundred yards of the summit. I was spent and nauseous and kept wanting to lie down and sleep, but Kipa was always at my side encouraging me. "*Ocolo, ocolo,*" he urged me on.

Meditator at sunset, along the Manang Trek

And then it was done. We cleared the summit. Too tired to shout or cheer or do a funny little pantomime, I simply lay down on the cold snow. Kipa put his arm around me and dragged me out of the wind to a pile of prayer stones where he gave me tea and biscuits. When I felt better, we embraced and laughed, and soon we headed down the other side into the Kali Gandaki River Valley.

A two-day descent brought us to the lowlands of Marfa and Ghasa. The forests and warmer climates were a welcome relief after three weeks in the high desert. We spent the night with an old hermit by the name of Tomba, a silent man who lived with his cat in a fallen-down house in the woods. There once had been a sign in front of his house offering overnight accommodations, but the painted letters had worn away long ago, and all that remained was a bare board. Tomba looked ethereal. He was tall and willowy, white-haired and gaunt-faced. Most of the time he was content to work in his garden or wander through the mountains looking for firewood. His prized possession was a tawny cat which he clutched in his thin arms.

Kipa and I enjoyed staying in his house. There was something refreshing in the man's monastic way of life. I envied him; he seemed happy with so very little. Sometimes we would work beside him in his garden pulling weeds and squashing insects. Once we climbed on top of his sagging roof and repaired it with new bamboo. At night Kipa liked to cook—big dishes of curried rice with dried yak meat, hot *dhal* (lentils) with garlic sauces, pan bread, and on one occasion, three bottles of beer that made Tomba grin like a schoolboy.

During our seven weeks on the trail, Kipa and I grew fond of the many porters we befriended along the way. These were hard-working, faithful men who carried enormous loads for miserable wages. We enjoyed spending time with them: sharing a meal in the forest out of the wind, treating their wounds with our first-aid kits, singing and dancing by their campfire in the evening. Often we rested together on the stone benches beneath the trees, catching our breath before clearing the next steep pitch of the trail.

In a village called Birethante Kipa and I once spent the whole evening with the porters, something I had always wanted to do. We heard singing and drumming from the far end of town and followed it through the streets until we came to a second-story loft. Climbing a ladder we entered a smoky room filled with people and animals, a magical space somewhere between a stable and a house. As in a scene from a Breughel painting, the porters sat in a circle, eating and drinking. An old *amma* in rags guarded the hearth and ladled out heaping portions of the steaming *tukpa*. Her two pretty daughters distributed glasses of *chiang* from earthen crocks. Three nanny goats lay sleeping on straw by a manger, and a handful of fat babies lay sleeping in blankets in a smaller loft above the manger.

This was the barn where the porters slept. As we entered, they made room for us in the circle. Several young men recognized us and waved to us to come and sit by them. Food and drink were passed our way—strong *chiang* and a plate of food that was unfamiliar to me. Kipa laughed and told me that it was coagulated sheep's blood and goat's feet. For a split second I hesitated, but then I merely said a prayer and began to eat. It tasted very good.

Kipa was soon dancing like a dervish. He had found another Sherpa in the room, and the two of them were swinging each other about the room to the driving music of flutes and drums. I got up from the circle and had a midnight spin with three different partners: a squat Magar man with a dark, woolly beard; a tall, thin Chetri man in a soiled, white tunic; and a Gurung man who tried to teach me a Cossack-type dance that nearly sent me through the rafters on one wild swing.

The *chiang* and the goat's feet kept coming all night long, as did the wild music, singing, and dancing. Sometime after midnight, porters began cheering for an American tune, and because so much of their music reminded me of Detroit motown music, I decided to give them a rousing rendition of a Smokey Robinson and the Miracles tune, "Tracks of My Tears," which brought the porters to their feet. When they yelled "Encore!" in Nepalese, I sang it again with a couple of John Travolta moves they really liked.

When the roosters began to crow, Kipa and I said good-bye to the porters and descended the ladder to the street below. Drunk, sweaty, and enormously happy, Kipa and I staggered home. Somewhere in the dark streets we stumbled on a sleeping yak who allowed our bungling to go unnoticed. Picking ourselves off the sleeping beast, we staggered on, laughing and shhhhhhing each other all the way to our tent. We somehow found our camp and climbed inside our sleeping bags without taking off our boots and clothes. While falling off to sleep, I distinctly heard Kipa humming the Smokey Robinson tune.

A week later we were back in Kathmandu. Our planned celebration at a Tibetan restaurant seemed inappropriate and was abandoned when we saw long lines of tourists waiting to get in. We shrugged our shoulders and moved drearily through the rain and crowded streets. But coming upon another restaurant, we decided to give it a try. It was a rather imposing, fancy restaurant that catered to rich tourists. The head waiter looked at us in a condescending manner and proceeded to give us a table in the rear. We were silent, somewhat dismayed, and waited uncomfortably for our meal. Kipa's beautiful eyes were sad and downcast. I saw him poking a disinterested finger at the folded cloth napkin on the china plate.

Our dinner arrived and was thrown down rudely by the waiter. Kipa struggled with the chicken, trying to use a knife and fork to cut the tough old bird. When I told him that I thought the chicken had probably walked over the Thorong La Pass, he laughed like the old Kipa. He looked at me, straight into my eyes, as if he was waiting for me to do something. In a sweeping gesture, I brushed away the silverware and picked the chicken up in my hands, attacking it with lip-smacking sounds, my elbows proudly on the table. Kipa joyfully followed in spite of looks from the head waiter and the fancy clientele. Coming out of the restaurant arm in arm, we raised our fists in the air and shouted and cheered for our triumph in completing the trek.

We took a taxi to the airport the following morning. We were silent the entire way. We had been inseparable for the past two months, and now we were to be yanked apart. There was great sadness in us both. My baggage was checked, my ticket cleared, and an announcement on the loudspeaker detailed the boarding procedure. It was time to go. We simply stood there looking at each other, eyes welling up with tears, not knowing what to say or do. As the final boarding was announced, Kipa reached into his parka and brought out a small tube wrapped in newspaper. He unfurled it carefully and brought out a *katak*, the beautiful white silk scarf traditionally given to a teacher or honored person. As tears streamed down both our faces, he carefully draped the scarf over my shoulders and embraced me, holding on to my lapels with clenched fists. Then he was gone, swallowed up in the crowd. I remained standing as he left me, crying and laughing with the crowds buzzing past me, until a flight attendant shook me from my trance and led me to the gate and the departing plane.

Storm clouds over Lake Petén Itzá

LAKE PETÉN ITZÁ

In the winter of 1982 I lived in an Indian village in the rain forests of Guatemala. The village was called San José and lay far to the north in the Petén province. Most of the villagers were Mayan Indians, descendants of the great pyramid builders of Mesoamerica. They grew crops of corn and beans and fished in the blue-green waters from dugout canoes. Many of the villagers still spoke Mayan.

San José was an ancient village of thatched houses on a hillside overlooking Petén Itzá, the largest lake in northern Guatemala—forty miles from end to end. Don Domingo, one of the oldest and most respected elders of the village, told me that San José was 850 years old. I believed him. The children were forever bringing me presents of *caritas* (little faces), small stone carvings of warriors, demon gods, and monkey priests they found in the forest.

During my first week in San José, I bought an old thatched cottage from a retired gum harvester who no longer lived there. The roof leaked, the walls were caving in, and at night giant cockroaches trudged across the dirt floors like sluggish gladiators. I cooked on the ground in a fire pit with dry jungle wood my neighbors gave me as a present. It was a typical Mayan house: mud, skinned poles, and beam rafters lashed together with vines and grass. At night I heard rats scurrying about in the dry thatch of the roof. It was not a house my father would sleep in, but I liked it. From my kitchen window I could gaze out at the lake and watch the villagers paddling their dugouts down to market. In the evenings I could sit on my doorstep and watch the men returning from their small garden plots in the jungle with machetes at their sides. Small boys dressed in white, barefoot and proud, led donkeys and mules carrying heavy sacks of corn and beans. This was an event that had occured nightly here for hundreds of

Early morning on the lake

years, with the creaking saddles, the strong smell of horse lather and sweat, and the rising dust.

To some extent it was still the 1920s in San José, give or take a few Bruce Springsteen T-shirts and Tupperware containers. Electricity had not yet arrived. People still drank from and bathed in the lake, and most were still happy to use the traditional dugout canoe. A new road was bulldozed a few years back, and a handful of trucks and cars had appeared. For the most part the villagers were either too poor or too stubborn to give up the boats of their ancestors in exchange for a piece of tin from Japan that ate gasolina. The shorelines were lined with these sleek wooden canoes which were still made in San José. There was an old canoe maker in the village, a bearded, solemn man who wore shredded huarache sandals and a burlap smock. I saw him in the jungle a number of times, felling giant cedar trees with a crude ax and then scooping out the insides with fire and an adz. When finished, the canoe weighed more than four hundred pounds and required a team of stout oxen to drag it out of the forest and down to the lake.

One of the easiest ways to meet the villagers was by shopping at the village stores. I think there were thirteen in all: Tienda de Graciela, Tienda de Rosa, and so on. They were hardly stores at all, more like little anterooms in homes where candles burned late at night. Sleepy shopkeepers dozed with their heads in their hands until someone came to ask for an egg, or a can of milk, or a box of matches.

For my bigger shopping, I went to Flores once a week, catching a ride down and back on the mail boat or on one of the intermittent motor launches. It was a beautiful ride along a forested shoreline where women and children bathed. San Andrés, San Benito, San Miguel drifted by at seven miles per hour. There was an adventurous feeling to the trip, with the men and women wearing colorful dress, and the children leaning over and dragging their hands in the water. Squealing pigs, raucus chickens, and piles of fruit and vegetables covered the deck. For some reason I had trouble getting aboard on time. I usually appeared at the very last second on the jetty, my too-long hair blowing about, ripped jeans sliding off my hips, bare feet slipping on the wet gunwales. If all the seats were taken and I had to squeeze next to a woman, everyone in the boat went "Eeeeeeeiiiiiii" all at once and then laughed.

There were four or five motor launches that came up the twenty miles from Flores to serve the people of San José, beautiful old-fashioned boats like those in *African Queen*—boats with tin roofs, long wooden benches, and paintings of phantoms and jungle beasts on the sides. My favorite was a sleek craft called *El Tigre*, owned and operated by a husky athlete (the champion boxer of Flores) named Oscar. His neck was about the size of my waist. Whenever he had a layover in San José, Oscar came to my house and asked me to run with him in the hills. He was fiercely competitive and ran easily through the forest paths. We ran from two to four miles and, coming down off the last hill, jumped into the lake for a long swim. Soon after, we were on our way to Flores with thirty passengers. Oscar let me ride free in exchange for the use of my Sony Walkman and headphones. His favorite tapes were by the Beach Boys and the Beatles. Quite often, cruising along at high speed, Oscar left the controls and did a funny mariachi dance in the bow at the feet of an unsuspecting woman, while the boat made long, lazy circles.

Living in San José was like living in any small town, except for the dugout canoes and the jaguars on the trail. My conversations with Diego at the thatched post office were not very different from the ones I used to have with Buster at the post office in Craftsbury, Vermont. But sometimes, when the light was just right—as I watched a woman standing in her dugout canoe paddling through the lagoons at sunset or saw a young boy with a warrior's face running through the jungle with thatch on his back—I was dazzled by these people, descendants of the great Maya.

I spent a lot of time visiting with the older villagers. My favorites were Francisco and Fuljensia Tesecún, who lived nearby in a thicket of caoba trees. Francisco and Fuljensia spoke Mayan as their first language and they tried to teach it to me. I was not very good at it, but they did not seem to mind. "Te ee yos (how are you)?" she called out to me as I approached on the path. "Bee sha bel (I am fine)," I responded. I had been practicing in front of the mirror at my house for the past ten minutes. If I could not remember the correct words, I would sneak a look down at my hands where I had inked them onto my palms. If the children saw me doing this, they howled with delight.

Francisco Tesecún making
a hammock

Once or twice a week I shared a meal with Francisco and Fuljensia. They usually sent over one of their grandchildren to get me, a dreamy seven-year-old girl with the beautiful name of Amor Esperanza, (waiting for love). We walked silently, hand-in-hand along the jungle path. The leafy bushes brushed against us as we went, and long-plumed quetzal birds flew above us. The old couple waited for us, and then we all lingered outdoors in the evening calm to watch the sky go from pink to blue to violet while the waves crashed white on the beach. We had dinner by candlelight: rice, beans, squash, and a traditional Mayan dish called *bollos*—small bits of pork dipped in corn meal, cooked in a green leaf over hot coals. Fuljensia got up from the table from time to time to make fresh tortillas, her slender hands slapping the moist dough back and forth in a rapid motion. The corn meal hissed on the hot grate, and the smell of crisped bread filled the air. We ate easily with one another, and our talk was slow and gentle. A child came to lean against a grandparent, while the smaller ones in the corner, too afraid to draw near, stared at me in silence. I was the first white person they had ever seen.

Francisco and Fuljensia had four grown sons: Edigar, Edín, Rufino, and Alfonso. All were married and lived close by. Alfonso, the youngest, often stopped at my house in the early dawn hours to see if I wanted to go with him to the fields. I usually went because I liked the Tesecúns; besides, they were traditional Mayan farmers. They planted by the moon, poured blood over the new seed corn to insure fertility, and cleared the land with ancient tools: a digging stick, a grub hoe, and a wooden plow that was so old it could have been in a museum.

Clearing the land for the corn, beans, and potatoes was hot, exhausting work. The Tesecúns were too poor to own a tractor or a team of oxen, so they harnessed themselves in the leather traces and pulled the plow. It was desperate work, even in the cool, early morning hours. The four brothers, the old father, and I strained in the harness, our muscled backs and shoulders rising and dipping toward the ground. Our feet dug into the soil, and rivulets of sweat ran down our brown bodies. The wooden plow was dull and worn, and the furrows we made were crooked and shallow. After four hours of backbreaking work, we had cleared half of the plot. Francisco called a halt, and we staggered to the shade of a giant mahogony tree and

Alfonso Tesecún returning from his fields

collapsed like spent animals. Not long after, we ate the lunch that Fuljensia had packed in a wicker basket—rice and beans, day-old tortillas, a flask of water. We ate our meal slowly and thankfully, in silence, as we looked at egrets in the treetops. Near the end of the meal, Alfonso looked inside the wicker basket and reported that Fuljensia had packed an apple pie. I drew closer. Alfonso reached in and grabbed a brown vine and hurled it at me, yelling, "*Culebra*, (snake)!" as the wiggly vine landed on my chest. I jumped up and screamed, thrashed my arms about to untangle the thing, swore in English and bad Spanish, and ran fifty yards and back. The Tesecúns laughed until tears streamed down their faces.

I also liked to spend time with Gerónimo and Ilda Martínez and their four small children. They were not Mayan, but were from another tribe far to the south. They were very poor and lived in an abandoned, fallen-down house far from the healing waters of the lake. I had seen Ilda hauling fifty-pound cans of water up the steep hill on several occasions. Gerónimo seemed thankful to have a roof over their heads, but I knew that he worried about providing for his family. He was clever and somehow managed. Once I watched as he spied a sickly water bird at the edge of the lake. He carefully waded out and grabbed the bird, took out a piece of string from his pocket, and tied the bird to a nearby bush. When he returned from town that afternoon, he waded out into the water, untied the bird, tucked it under his arm, and took it home for his supper.

I often went hunting with Gerónimo on trails that crisscrossed the rain forests in a hundred directions. He was a true hunter, like the Eskimo of the tundra and the Bushmen of the Kalahari, lean and powerful and wary. The last time we hunted together was on the new moon of April. We left the village at dawn, hiking north out of town on a jungle trail that was eerie, bathed in long shadows. Even in the semidarkness, Gerónimo moved silently, with grace and precision. When the sun rose, looking like a red serpent over the carpeted hills, we were many miles from home. The jungle came to life: birds began to sing; insects took up their incessant droning in the bush; and two snakes, fat as my wrist, slithered across the trail and were gone.

Gerónimo carried a rifle, but he really hunted with his senses. I watched as he crouched and smelled the dank air, wafting handfuls to his nostrils with his hand, whispering, "*Venado* (deer)." He knew where an animal had walked two days before, and he knew what animal it had been. He bent to inspect splayed bunches of grasses like a bone specialist looking at a fracture on an x ray.

In the middle of the day, when the heat drove us to any available water, I watched as he drank from a murky water hole where all the jungle animals drank. He looked like an animal himself, slinking toward the coffee-colored water's edge, dropping down on all fours. Once during the drink he lifted his head and turned in all directions to see if he, too, was being watched.

At a low point in the hunt—tired, hungry, bug-infested, grumpy—I noticed a new look on Gerónimo's face. "¿Que pasa?" I asked. "Perdido," was all he said, a sly grin coming over his face. I wondered: *Perdido, perdido*, what the hell does *perdido* mean? Must come from the verb *peder*, to lose. *Perdido*, lost. Ah shit, we're lost! Gerónimo exploded into laughter and then swung out on the trail north toward the mountains. I followed.

By the middle of the day we had logged maybe seventeen long, dusty miles and had shot only one bird, a scrawny game hen called a chachalaca. We headed back to San José, and after several hours arrived by four o'clock. At the edge of town where our trails forked, his to the left, mine to the right, Gerónimo surprised me by offering me the chachalaca as a gift. "Para su cena (for your supper)," he said, handing me the bird. I naturally refused, but I was deeply touched by his generosity.

That night the stars shone like little fires above the lake, and the heat sat heavily on the village. I walked to a dilapidated house in town where a man often kept cold beer. The old fellow had an Electrolux fridge that ran on kerosene. His prices were high, but the beer was ice-cold. I bought six bottles. I hiked through the village on pathways that wound through thickets of trees and past the orange light that splashed out onto the trail from open-hearth flames. At the top of the hill Gerónimo and Ilda's hut came into view, bathed in moonlight. I found them outside, sitting quietly on the flat rocks like statues. They were happy to see me. I took a bottle of cold beer and laid it against Ilda's bare shoulder. She gasped. She was beside herself with joy. (Women in Guatemala were rarely treated as equals to men and so went without many luxuries.) We drank the beer and spent the

Boys visiting the author

evening watching shooting stars fall toward the lake below. Gerónimo toasted me with his second bottle and promised that we would go hunting again, that we would not get lost, and that the smallest thing we would bring home would be a deer. Ilda laughed at us both.

I started to build a dock at my beach that went almost forty feet out into the lake. The children began jumping off it even before it was finished. Four village men helped me: Gerónimo, Old Solomon, Isaro (my neighbor), and Isaias (pronounced Ee-sa-ee-as). We often took a fruit break in the late afternoon—bananas, mangos, pineapples—and sat in a circle, feet straight out in front of us, enjoying the breeze from the lake. Don Domingo, a village elder I had grown fond of, often stopped by and joined us. I loved to watch him as he peeled a pineapple with five easy swipes of his machete. Once we tried to throw the old man into the lake, but he ran away from us with spry old jumping-frog's legs, laughing as he disappeared into the jungle.

We finished the dock and all the children began to swim at my beach. The water was beautiful, soft and green and warm, almost slippery. The bottom was clear and sandy. I liked to swim out into the lake, a quarter mile and more, and let the hills, the thatched houses, and the tall white church come into view. I lay on my back and drifted in the calm water until small boys sneaked up on me, pinched my toes, and yelled, "*Aligador* (alligator)!".

Even though the children were forever around me, I seldom tired of them. There were hundreds of them, round-faced cherubs buzzing around my house, waiting for me at every bend in the trail. They called me don Luis for some reason, and often the diminutive, Huicho. ("Ethan" did not seem to work in Spanish.) There was another Huicho in the village, a six-year-old who belonged to Luis and Rosa. Often when I was down at the beach doing my dishes or bathing, the boy and I yelled back and forth to each other with great bullfrog voices: "HUICHO" . . . "HUICHO."

My house was always open to the children. They gathered around it like people at a movie, waiting for it to open. I did not mind as long as there were not more than thirty, although one day I had fifty. For most of the children, it was their first opportunity to be close to an outsider. Our houses were the same on the outside, but inside they were worlds apart. They were mesmerized by my wall hangings, especially two giant posters. One was of Sergeant Pepper's Lonely Hearts Club Band (the one with the four Beatles all duded up in red marching suits), and one was of King Kong climbing the Empire State Building and clutching a woman in his hand. "¿Don Huicho, es verdad (is it true)?" The children also adored my traveler's odds and ends, but my shaving kit was their favorite. They all went through it fifty times or more, and they never tired of it. "¿Que es este, don Huicho (what is this)?" they asked as they pulled out great spools of my dental floss. "Para dientes, niños (for your teeth, kids)." And then I did a little flossing pantomime that brought them to tears of laughter. The Swiss Army knife was also an intriguing item, although they were not allowed to open it by themselves. When I gave a presentation of all thirteen blades, an obedient silent circle formed to watch *the miracle*.

The mothers seemed happy my house was open to the children. On rainy days, when the jungle was awash in muck and mud, ten or twenty little ones spent the day at my house, stringing beads into necklaces and bracelets, coloring, or maybe working on a jigsaw puzzle. Often, I read them *Charlotte's Web, Peter Pan,* and Beatrix Potter's *The Tale of Peter Rabbit*. My Spanish was not very good, and I bungled a lot when translating the English into Spanish, but the children never complained. "O.K. niños, éste es *Las Adventuras de Conejo Pedro*. . . ."

Of all the children in the village, my two favorites were little sisters, Lyoda, seven, and Beti, five. They were the children of Alicia and Isaro, my closest neighbors. Because they lived so close—eleven feet to be exact—the girls were in my house every minute of every day, warbling like songbirds. When suppertime came and I shooed the children home to their parents, I always made exceptions for Lyoda and Beti. Then we had the whole house to ourselves. Little Beti went down to the lake and brought fresh water, and Lyoda did the dishes on the hearth. A hush descended on the cottage while the wind rustled the palms overhead and the waves crashed softly on the beach. We snuggled together on the bed, strung beads, and told jokes. Sometimes I read to them, long continuation stories of *Little Red Riding Hood* and *Snow White and the Seven Dwarfs*. Then Alicia's voice came, "Beti, Lyoda, venga, venga. Tiempo para dormir (come on, time for bed)." And they jumped up and kissed me goodnight and skipped out the door.

Many of the families in San José were kind to me. I was always coming home to find a bag of potatoes or squash, a bunch of bananas, or a basketful of mangos on my doorstep. And if I had been too busy to cook, some of the mothers sent over a pot of soup or some rice and beans. One mother regularly sent over a wicker basket of warm tortillas at suppertime, beautifully wrapped in a white cloth napkin, hand-embroidered with a scene from the village.

I reciprocated as best I could by making formal visits to their homes. The villagers seemed honored when I came to call. A chair was produced and the seat patted encouragingly, "Oh, don Huicho, pase adelante. Siéntese, siéntese, por favor (don Huicho, come over here. Sit down, sit down, please.)." The mother reheated the morning coffee on the fire. The old grandmother went and made fresh tortillas, her thin, muscled hands quick and dexterous. The father sat down and moved his hands back and forth together as he prepared to make conversation. I loved to ask them historical questions. When did the last medicine woman die? What was her name? What plants did she use? The old grandmother piped up from her seat by the fire if the parents did not know the answer to my question.

On these visits children were not permitted to sit with us, let alone rumpus as they did down at my house. They stood in the bedroom, five or six abreast, heads sticking out, eyes bulging. If for a single second I glanced in their direction, I could feel the love in their dancing eyes and mischievous smiles. It was best not to look, or the parents would get mad. At the end of the visit the father often walked me to my home, slowly like a grandfather, stopping under the palms to look out at the lake or up at the night sky.

There were many eligible young women in San José. Handsome, long-haired beauties in their early twenties regularly paraded around the town square in the evening, usually in a protective group of five or six, in their best dresses and high-heeled shoes. They pretended they were just taking the night air, but they were actually looking for husbands. I never knew whether I fit into their scheme of things. Probably not. I was just an old hippie who lived in Cornelio Chable's fallen-down house. When they passed me on their rounds, I heard them twittering and giggling. God only knows what they said among themselves.

Holy communion

82 *Lake Petén Itzá*

Costura, a friend

84 *Lake Petén Itzá*

There was a young woman, however, whom I saw from time to time, a beautiful twenty-year-old by the name of Norma Aurora. She did my laundry, and so once or twice a week I had a fine excuse to go to her house to see her. When I knocked on the door, her grandmother, the old midwife for San José, greeted me warmly and called down to the beach for Norma. "Norma, Norma, el señor esta aquí, venga (the gentleman is here, come along)." Norma came running up, her long black hair falling loosely about her shoulders, her eyes dark and fiery. The grandmother allowed us to walk together along the beach where we sat and talked. The old woman did not permit laundry visits at night, however.

On my final day in San José, I took my last climb up the hill, past Gerónimo and Ilda's house to a high, grassy knoll overlooking the full forty miles of the lake. There, with the trade winds blowing and the late afternoon sun shining yellow-green on the jungle below, I sat for almost an hour and dreamt of the time when the highest civilization in all the Americas had stretched out below. It had been a time of great energy, when priests and astronomers controlled the daily lives of the Maya. Warriors traveled the jungle pathways, sacrifices fell from the temple heights, and cities of white stone rose in rain forest clearings. The little village below me, San José, was one of the last living vestiges of the great Mayan puzzle.

Sister shepherdesses, above
Sumdo (16,000 feet)

LAND OF THE BROKEN MOON

In 1983 I spent the early autumn with a Muslim family on a Victorian houseboat on Kashmir's Dal Lake. I slept and bathed on an adjacent boat called *Light House*, but took my meals with the family on their boat. We ate spicy Mogul food—fiery curries in earthen bowls and lamb that we would eat with our fingers. Early morning was my favorite time of day. The grandmother, a large-boned woman with marvelously calloused feet, fed white chickens on the spit of land that eased out to the boats. Haji, the family patriarch, and his older brother drank strong coffee and smoked a hubble-bubble, great clouds rising about them. The children readied themselves for school: the boys wore crisp blue shorts, the girls, white saris. The family boatman, a toothless old man in rags, paddled them to the shore in a pencil-thin boat called a *shikara*. Egrets circled in the blue skies, white against the mountains rising to the north.

Winter was coming on. Poplars glowed like coals on the slopes above the lake, and fresh snow was on the mountains. On October 1st I said good-bye to my houseboat family and boarded a tiny two-engine plane in Srinagar for Ladakh, flying over the highest mountains in the world. Below me I saw a vast white kingdom of glaciers and unmapped valleys, a no-man's-land of frost and bitter cold and shrieking winds. A half hour later we landed in Leh on a tiny cobble runway at eleven thousand feet. My first impression was that we had landed on another planet.

Indeed, Ladakh was other-worldly. The local people called it "the land of the broken moon." Leh had once served as a crossroad trading center on the east-west silk and spice routes. A medieval mood lingered here; there were caravans, pony trains, and pilgrims, all bound for the Holy Land. In the center of the city loomed the Old Palace, a miniature Lhasa built on the side of a mountain. At night the

Tsetan, near Marka

cobbled streets were deserted, and the air was heavy with the sweet smell of burning juniper.

I stayed the first week in a guesthouse called Otsal Cottage. The owner, Mr. Sonam, put me in an annex with a young Tibetan lama and his sister. In the morning I meditated with them in their small room as the sun streamed in through a tiny window. Through Mr. Sonam I learned of a Tibetan pony-man living in a nearby refugee camp who was willing to take me into the Himalayas for several weeks of trekking. Ladakh had only opened its borders to Westerners in 1974, and I was anxious to see this last stand of Tibetan Buddhism before it changed. Tibet, its neighbor to the north, had been ravaged by the Chinese Army during the Cultural Revolution. Temples and monasteries were destroyed, and the continuum of devotional practices ruptured and perhaps lost to an entire generation.

I first met Nono Tsetan at his refugee camp some twelve miles north of Leh. He was a strong man in his thirties, typical of those Tibetans who still worked the land. When I met him, he was sitting in the noon sun, cross-legged on a pile of saddle pads, mending a worn saddle with needle and thread. We greeted each other in the traditional Ladakhi manner, *"Jullay"*. . . *"Jullay,"* with our hands clasped in a prayerful pose, the Buddha meeting the Buddha. We sat together on the ground talking as best we could. His wife, a hearty, robust woman, served us Tibetan salt tea. Soon afterward we were at work laying out provisions for the trek. There were bags of potatoes and carrots, sweet onions and garlic, rice, bulgur, tea, dried fruit, cooking oil, a kerosene stove, blankets, and horse equipment. Before our departure, Tsetan's eight children came out to embrace their father. For a brief moment in that sad refugee camp, the family stood as a symbol of the cohesive force of Tibetan body, spirit, and mind. We next loaded two strong little horses and headed north toward the White Mountains.

Tsetan wore a floppy woolen cap and long cloaks tied together with sashes. He was always playing with his long black pigtails, and his skin was red-black from years at high altitudes. He had a long black mustache and a long, pointed, wispy chin beard. He was a magical-looking man, a cross between a laughing Buddha and reggae singer Bob Marley. While walking, Tsetan liked to keep busy, and he would

tie the reins about his waist and spin yarn from a clump of wool inside his cloak. When he returned, his wife would knit socks for the children. He kept an old, large, portable radio under his cloaks as well, a possession he prized above all others. From time to time, batteries permitting, he would listen to the news about Lhasa on Radio Tibet, to chants and chimes, and sometimes to the Dalai Lama himself.

On the first day the trail passed through a tiny settlement called Sumdo. It was a dusty grouping of four adobe houses beside a dry wash that supported a grove of aspen and poplar trees, a rarity in this harsh and barren landscape. There is less rain in Ladakh than in the Sahara Desert. Tsetan introduced me to the village *amchi* (doctor), a man in his fifties who had studied medicine in Tibet for four years. He was the sixth *amchi* of the village, and was training his grandson, a boy of eleven, to be the seventh. We were escorted into their small home, still cool from the night, where he served us tea and walnuts. He showed us the clothbound medical books, fragile and sere, from which he had received his teachings. He said that they were five hundred years old.

Farther along the trail, climbing upward on a steep, stony hill, we came to an ominous-looking hole in the ground. Tsetan explained that it was a wolf trap. The villagers would stake a weakened goat to a post at the bottom, and when the wolf came to make the kill a sliding trap door would ensnare it. In this harsh landscape a single wolf could spell the difference between a winter of plenty and one of scarcity.

We arrived at a small settlement at dusk, a deep cold descending on us from the mountains. We stayed with a family of eleven whom Tsetan knew—a ragged group in coarse garments that smelled of yak wool and wood smoke. Tsetan and the father began talking as they unloaded the horses. The children circled around me, touching my white skin and staring at my blue eyes.

The father seemed particularly eager to show me the meditation hall on the third story. It was a formal room: embroidered cushions on a red lacquered floor, tapestries and *thangkas* on the walls, bells, chimes, statues, prayer flags, and a fine library of clothbound Tibetan Buddhist volumes. Wintertime, he explained as we crawled down a ladder, was the season when people poured themselves into their devotional practice.

That night we all gathered in the tiny kitchen for the evening meal: the shiny-faced children, the mother and father in their black velvet frocks, a toothless and happy old wood gatherer from a neighboring valley, and Tsetan and me. The *amma* served *tukpa*, *tsampa* (bread), and *mo mo* (meat pies)— delicious food. We ate with our fingers, kneading the mushy barley and slurping it into our mouths. Slurping one's food was considered proper etiquette, a high compliment to the host. Beside the open hearth fire we slurped away to our heart's content.

Next morning at dawn, when the high desert was bathed in a pink and yellow light, the *amma* left for the valley with five small donkeys loaded with wool. Her eleven-year-old son accompanied her, as did the wood gatherer in his ragged cloak and torn cloth shoes. Tsetan and I departed on the same path an hour later, climbing up through yellow desert canyons that were bitterly cold and tomb-like where the sun had not yet appeared. Nearing fourteen thousand feet on a twisting, narrow cliff trail, we suddenly came upon our friends. One of the small donkeys was thrashing about, braying mournfully, its back hind leg wedged between two boulders. Tsetan was at the animal's side in seconds, unstrapping its load like a rodeo star. He wrestled the poor beast to safety. Soon afterward, we were traveling again, this time as a group, climbing towards the seventeen-thousand-foot pass and Mingiling Glacier.

In the early afternoon, at close to sixteen thousand feet, we rested on the cold slopes of scree and thin grass and let the animals graze. The *amma* saw I was having difficulty with the steep pitch of the trail and the high elevations and waved to me as encouragement. She held up a flask of tea to prompt me along. Ten minutes later I drew close and crawled the last twenty yards on my belly in a funny little pantomime that made everyone laugh. The *amma* gave me thick slices of dark bread with sweet butter and a flask of strong Tibetan salt tea. An hour later we cleared the summit and celebrated the safe journey with a "hip-hip-hooray" in Ladakhi, and the small boy pinned a prayer flag to a staff in the rocks.

Several days later Tsetan and I came to a windy plain. At sixteen thousand feet there were no villages, only the wind, the cold, and occasional shepherds' huts—crude chambers with three-foot-thick stone walls. We stayed two nights at one of these encampments with

Ladakhi couple with grandson

a family of poor shepherds from the lowlands, the last people to be out in the mountains with their herds at this late season. Their two-room hut had hides on the roof. Carcasses of sheep and goats were drying in the sun, and lean dogs were slinking about. The family consisted of two grandparents, old-timers with smudgy faces; a father with long hair and a woolly beard; a mother in skins who milked the yaks and sang low moaning chants; three strong brothers who rode fast horses across the dusty plains; and five beautiful daughters with long black hair and flashing smiles. They fed us roast yak and turnips for supper. At night I rested on a pile of sheepskins in the corner of the hut, and every time someone came into the smoky room dressed in rags and skins, I swore I had been transported to another time. Before drifting off to sleep that first night, I brought out small gifts for the family: needles for the mother, safety pins for the grandmother, razor blades for the men, and colorful balloons and small tins of Nivea cream for the daughters. In turn, two of the sisters heated bear oil on the fire and gave me a hot oil scalp treatment that brought Tsetan to tears of laughter.

Days later we passed through softer, greener valleys at lower elevations. In a town named Hankar, we passed villagers dressed in traditional costumes at work harvesting food. I lay down at the edge of a field and slept in the warm autumn sunshine. I was awakened by a woman and her baby who had come with a handful of peas. We sat together for a time, shelling peas, the baby staring at me with wide eyes.

Tsetan and I traveled like desert nomads, putting in long, hard days between villages. We walked down winding canyons and dry riverbeds, from one valley to another. I was feeling strong and hard, my face was dark and peeling, and the muscles in my body were tough and lean. The cold at night did not seem to bother me as once it had. Tsetan had given me an old horse blanket to wear, and I seemed to fit into the landscape.

We spent nearly a week in a village called Marka, with a thousand-year-old citadel perched on a cliff overlooking a small valley of barley and wheat fields. Marka, close to fourteen thousand feet, was a Buddhist village. A large *gompa* (monastery) dominated the village, and its white turrets and domes and snapping prayer flags rose high

above all else. It was harvest time, and most of the villagers (children included) were at work in the fields with hand scythes and long knives, cutting golden barley from the stalks and drying it in the sun. Barley was their staff of life: bread, noodles, cereals, desserts, even their beer came from the grain.

While in Marka, we stayed with a Tibetan family, sleeping in a room over the yak stable where saddles and sacks of grain were stored. There were the smells of uninterrupted centuries there: barley chaff and yak dung, horse lather and smoked meats. At night, when the wind tore at the roof, Tsetan and I went to sleep by candlelight, warm and secure, curled up in a mound of horse blankets.

The children of Marka were enchanting. I used to love to spend time with them, playing jacks on the flat rocks by the monastery, or flying paper kites no bigger than leaves in the cloudless blue skies. Sometimes we would play frisbee together down by the river, where they tended their sheep and goats. I often held their chapped little hands as we went, hands that felt like rough iron. These mountain people rarely bathed or washed their hair, as the climate was too cold. I always carried a tin of Nivea cream and would rub their faces with it, looking into their eyes and speaking softly to them all the while.

Tsetan and I worked beside the villagers in the fields, harvesting barley. I found joy in this work: in the golden grain that shone in the sun, in the singing that rose from all corners of the field. The men chanted one long chorus, and the women and children sang a sweet refrain. These were songs, chants, and rounds centuries old. Sometimes during the day the resident lama wandered down from the hill to visit. We formed a circle around him and shared a bottle or two of *chiang*. Tsetan was at his best on these occasions, performer and mischief-maker. He got tipsy on the brew and told story after story. His arms flew out in exclamation at an important part of the story, and his sly, magical eyes narrowed down to tiny slits for the scary part. People adored him wherever we went. Even the lama, a holy man, found him irresistable.

Sometimes in the late afternoon, when long rows of drying grain made the land look neat and orderly, I lay on my sleeping bag at the edge of the fields and wrote in my journal. I recorded my thoughts about travel, about the similarities and differences among people of

Harvesting barley near Hankar
(15,000 feet)

the world. Many of the villagers, especially the older people, were strangely intrigued by my books, pens, paper, and journals; it was as if I had been a wizard from another land. One old man in pigtails used to sit close to me with a prayer wheel as I wrote. Once he asked me what my name was and where I lived. I wrote on a piece of paper, "Ethan Hubbard from America," and handed it to him. He held it in his rough hands, eyebrows arched inquisitively, repeating over and over, "America, America," as if he could in this way determine how many mountain ranges lay between us and my home.

We left Marka and our Tibetan family one cold October morning, and the lama invited Tsetan and me into his tiny cell for a final cup of tea. Down river we went through a lonely and desolate valley that had been ravaged by a recent flood. Boulders the size of houses lay scattered on the fallow fields. Nearby there was a village of rickety buildings perched on the chalky cliffs. We stopped and visited with an old woman in rags and bare feet who was chopping wood beside her small house. Her black dog snarled at us the whole time. She was a desperate, poor soul who seemed worn out. She kept asking us to buy a bottle of beer from her, which we eventually did, and then we moved on down the valley.

Later that afternoon, Tsetan and I got drunk on that bottle of beer. We ran helter-skelter down the valley, hooting and hollering and carrying on, and the horses frolicked after us with their reins dragging on the ground. Tsetan surprised me by crossing a swollen river on one of the horses, laughing as he rode it backward through the rapids. He came back to get me, gathered me up in his strong arms, and took me to the other side where we made a fire and fell asleep in a pile of leaves on the ground.

It was late October and it began to snow, not much, but enough to make getting up in the morning uncomfortable. At night it was often below zero. If a cloud passed in front of the sun, the temperature plummeted twenty degrees in a matter of minutes. We saw hunters, lean hungry men with searching eyes, who rode fast ponies. Winter was coming on, and they were making last minute preparations.

We traveled through high valleys strewn with boulders where eagles and vultures soared in the dull wintry skies. Jagged peaks rose into the snow clouds. For several days we climbed up along a mountain trail without seeing anyone, sleeping at night by a small fire that

Ladakhi father with son

we made with dried yak dung. There was a harsh beauty to this part of the trek: in the biting wind that tore at our faces, in the courage and stamina of our little horses, and in our silence as we lay close together in our blankets at night.

Not far from the Gonalung Pass, we came to a large villa at fifteen thousand feet called Shing-O. There were two matriarchal grand-mothers (sisters, I believe) who allowed us to sleep on the third floor in the granary. It was good to be out of the cold. I welcomed the opportunity to sit by the hearth fire in the smoky kitchen as the old women went about their work. They were very kind to me and fed me Tibetan fried bread and strong salt tea with rancid yak butter. We talked as I ate, each in our own language, but I did not care what was said. It felt wonderful to be in a warm family kitchen.

There were two young sisters at Shing-O who harvested root crops in a small garden by the stable. I watched them from afar, drawing close when I felt that they had accepted my presence. For several afternoons as the sun fell on us, we pulled carrots and smooth-skinned potatoes from the cold ground. The decayed smell of the black composted soil was thick and yeasty in the air. Sometimes we inched close to one another, with our fingers deliciously brushing together, and our breath faintly warming each other's neck or cheek. Sometimes I threw a smooth round stone into the collecting basket and pretended that it was a potato. The beautiful sisters erupted into laughter and chastised me by slapping my hand.

A few days later we were back on the trail heading over Gonalung Pass. I found this to be an austere and lonely part of the journey, especially after sharing those sweet times with the young sisters at Shing-O. The wind and snow blew harder each day, ripping and tearing at us, sometimes throwing me down on the ground like chaff. Tsetan kept his spirits up and seemed undaunted by the bleakness of it all, encouraging me with his knowing, mystical smile.

We passed a string of dirty, unfriendly settlements in the lower valleys, hardscrabble villages with brutish-looking people. Huge guard dogs on sturdy chains lunged at us as we passed. A man in a red robe scurried across the hillside above us and was gone. We headed down a steep canyon that brought us to a small village called Zing Chen. Tsetan stretched out on the jagged rubble with his usual abandonment and was soon fast asleep. Out of nowhere an old man

Schoolboy hauling barley,
near Sumdo

Monastery outside Leh

in rags appeared with a handful of poppies. He begged me to come with him to his little house, where he showed me his garden and fruit trees. He brought me to his altar inside where there was a wooden Buddha, a picture of the Dalai Lama, and a vase where he placed the orange flowers.

We stayed over with the poppy man, and Tsetan and I shared his stable loft. This was our last night together on the trail. Tomorrow we would be down in the Indus Valley, close to Leh. I had been paying Tsetan a daily wage for his services, money that he squirreled away in a sock in his cloak. I was forever trying to steal it back, a joke we never tired of. But I wanted to give him a bonus, a gift. That night I asked him to sit quietly on the bed with his eyes closed as I arranged before him a three-piece stainless-steel cooking set—an object of particular fascination. Inside the third pot I hid twenty-five dollars. When he opened his eyes, he was overwhelmed and cried, his tears falling unabashedly.

That night Tsetan tried to talk to me in English for the very first time. He labored with the words, his face contorted and his eyes pleading. I think he tried to tell me that next year, if I came back, he would take me into a distant kingdom called Zanskar.

In the morning we parted, Tsetan heading north along the Indus River to his refugee camp and his family, and I, west to Leh and a reunion with Mr. Sonan at the Otsal Cottage. Our parting was brief. I think we both understood that there was no way to express our feelings. We hugged and squeezed one another, great bear hugs full of lovely groans and laughter. While hugging I tried to steal Tsetan's money bag inside his cloak, and we howled with delight. And then we were separated. The wind blew cold across the dry plain, moving dark clouds through the sky.

A week later, rested, clean, and fat from eating Chinese food at my favorite restaurant in Leh, I was overjoyed to find Tsetan in my upstairs room at the Otsal Cottage. He had walked the twelve miles from his refugee camp to bring me a present, a handsomely woven satchel that he had made from the wool he had spun during our trip. He grinned and told me to look inside the bag. I rummaged around and discovered a six-sided quartz crystal. We sat on my bed holding hands, his familiar smile and squinty eyes openly showing me his love. Then he left. In my heart I knew I would never see him again.

Cattle station, Ororoo (South Australia)

ORROROO AND DOWN UNDER

In January 1983 I arrived in Sydney in sweltering summer heat and took a room at a small hotel on a quiet side street near Kings Cross Station. For the next several days I explored the city on foot, long hauls of five and six hours that took me to the very edges of the city. Of all the things I saw—The Opera House, the harbor and dockyards, fancy shops along the bay—a scene I witnessed in a small park near my hotel affected me the most. Drunk and disheveled old men came each day to sprawl out on the grass and drink themselves into a stupor. Though deeply saddened by the sight of those lonely men, I was moved even more by a beautiful young nun in white who appeared every morning on a motor scooter to wash and shave each of the men. I watched her as she heated hot water on a portable stove and applied lather to their craggy faces, speaking softly as she worked.

While in Sydney, I rented a motorcycle from a dealer. It was a Yamaha 250 XT, a road-and-dirt bike, with a milk crate on the back to carry my camping gear and billy can. (The man who rented me the bike said that good Australian travelers always carried a billy can to brew their tea.) On a hot January morning I headed into the Blue Mountains of New South Wales.

For several weeks I traveled aimlessly through sheep and cattle country, along dusty roads and dry creek beds, passing through villages and valleys. Wheat-colored hills, giant gum trees in tall grasses, and low mountains sloping to the west rolled gently by. Small farming communities dotted the countryside, and their architecture made me think of what America must have looked like fifty years ago. During the day I stopped and visited with farmers and ranchers in their fields and barnyards. They were friendly and talkative and seemed to have more questions about America than I did about Australia.

I spent a week in the mountains up around Bathurst in a gold mining village called Hill End, a turn-of-the-century place with white clapboard houses and a dirt main street. The men of the village still mined gold with picks and shovels. There was a pub in Hill End where, in the heat of the day, swagmen, bounty riders, miners, and jackeroos gathered to chase the dust from their throats with tall pitchers of cold beer. I enjoyed drinking with them. Their thick accents, lined faces, and slouched hats made me feel like I was living in another time.

One old swagman named Ned Doughterty used to take me home after we had shared a pitcher or two. Ned was kind and generous, and when not tending his sheep, he made sure I was well taken care of. He let me sleep on his property by a slow-moving creek in a forest of gum trees. It was a long walk down a bridle trail to the creek, but the setting was primordial and enchanting. Rosy-breasted parrots called out in the dusk, the light from my campfire pulsed on the smooth-barked limbs of the gum and eucalyptus trees, and the new moon and a handful of bright stars shone softly through the leafy branches.

One night near dusk, as I was washing my dishes down at the creek, a family of kangaroos came to drink on the opposite shore. At first they were frightened by my presence and nearly turned and hopped away. But then they found their courage and stayed, bending down gracefully to drink. When the kangaroos had finished drinking, they rose up and stared at me benignly for several long still moments. The breeze moved gently through the broad-leafed plants on the shore, and the setting sun was reflected on the ripples in the water. We looked at one another for a minute or two with fascination, and then slowly they turned and made their way back into the forest.

That evening after supper I curled up at the base of a giant gum tree in a pile of leaves, listened to the forest sounds, and watched the stars appear in the sky. The world took on new dimensions that night and the details of my surroundings were subtly, but perceptibly enlarged. The night shadows from my fire seemed longer and more mysterious, the sounds of tree frogs and cicadas more alluring. The air was heavy with the sweet fragrance of orchids and ferns. Firelight danced on my naked skin, and I felt charged with an earthy power, as if the forest and the creek and the kangaroos were an integral part of my life.

I had wanted to see the Aborigines, the original Australians who, like myself, had spent days and nights down at Ned's creek listening to night sounds around a fire. Perhaps they, too, had watched a family of kangaroos come to drink there. So, one morning I decided to head for Alice Springs, in the center of the desert outback, where I had been told I could see all the Aborigines I wanted.

Flying low over the continent from Sydney to Alice Springs, I saw mountain ranges, red-orange and black, stretching as far as the eye could see. The desert floor sprawled out to the west—dotted with intermittent mining roads, cattle, and sheep stations. Three hours later we landed in Alice Springs. Coming off the plane I was immediately aware of being in the middle of a vast desert. In the shade the temperature read 110 degrees. Beyond the fences of the airport lay jagged mountains that seemed to bleed in the afternoon heat, and yellow earth lay all around me, barren and cracked. We boarded an air-conditioned shuttle bus that sealed us off from the desert we had come to see.

On the way into town I saw the Aborigines. They sat in small circles, as still as statues in the tall grass under shade trees. Even from the window of the speeding bus they looked shockingly poor. They were shoeless and wore ragged clothes. There was a ghost-like quality about them; it was as if their bodies were still there, but their souls had long since vanished. I had the feeling that something monumental—disasterous—had happened to them. I sat at the edge of my seat and stared. No one else on the bus seemed to notice them.

Alice Springs was a modern city of twenty thousand people in the heart of the desert outback. Once an important cattle and mining center for the country's interior, it was now a major tourist center that catered to the wealthy traveler. People came from all over the world to see the desert outback: the quintessence of nothingness. The hardpan soil, blistering sands, blazing heat, and huge ominous sky seemed to fill tourists with wonder and make them thankful for their own cozy little niches back home in Germany or Yugoslavia.

Long before cattle and mining—all the way back to the last ice age—Alice Springs had belonged to the Aborigines of the western desert. It had been the holiest of their holy shrines, the very source of their game and water, the inspiration for their myths and ceremonies.

Aborigne men, Alice Springs (Northern Territory)

But their land had been torn from them. Signs in store fronts in Alice Springs read: Proper Dress Code Enforced For Admittance: Pressed Pants And Collared Shirts. This local ordinance single-handedly disqualified most of Alice Springs' fifteen hundred Aborigines from even the most basic of civil rights. They were outcasts in their own land.

I took a room in the local YMCA at the edge of town. The Australians who ran the hostel, a gentle couple by the name of Petra and Peter, invited me up to their apartment the first night for supper and talk. They were kind and shared what they knew of the Aborigines, giving me pointers on how I might go about meeting some of them. They also loaned me their bicycle for the duration of my stay.

The following morning in a stifling heat, I rode around the outskirts of Alice Springs and got my first glimpse of the encampments that ringed the city. They were grim places, hardscrabble camps of cardboard and tin where Aborigines lived in tribal and family bands. Most were from nearby tribes like the Anmatjera or the Warlpiri and were trying to get back home to their reserves. Some were waiting to be admitted to the hospital. Others had no hope of going anywhere.

There was a desperation in the camps. At night the women got drunk on sickeningly-sweet sherry and brawled in the streets, bashing and clubbing each other. During the day bands of hungry-looking men in rags roamed the city with a look of insurrection on their faces. In the groves where their families camped, babies screamed in the searing heat: neglected, hungry, and often dehydrated. Parents were too drunk to remember they even had a child. Weary old men sat in circles, eating gristly meat and gnashing bones they had scavenged from garbage cans at the slaughterhouse on the other side of town.

I began to go see the Aborigines on my bicycle every day. I took long rides around the edge of the city that took me to Hoppy's Camp, Three Mile Junction, and a sacred stone outcropping called the Howling Dingo Monument (once a major shrine to these desert people). At first the Aborigines did not know what to make of a white man coming to see them. But they did allow me to sit with them around their campfires at night, and on their stone piles in the shade during the day. I watched silently as old men carved boomerangs and worked stone into spearpoints that would never be used. Sometimes the old men and women taught the children how to paint the enigmatic designs of their ancestors. These fiery whorls and scrolls alluded perhaps to dream states that revealed the location of water or knowledge of the soul of an animal they intended to kill. The Aborigines spoke no English, so we communicated with each other with a handshake or a smile or laughter. Day after day I arrived and took interest in their lives, and slowly, ever so slowly, a feeling of trust and friendship developed between us.

When I saw how malnourished and hungry they were, I began carrying a knapsack full of food: cheese and sandwich meats, fruit and yogurt, cold milk for the dehydrated babies, tea and biscuits for the old men. Sometimes when I brought a carton of eggs for the group, the men and I made a fire of sticks and hard-boiled them in billy cans. Bringing food, of course, was only a gesture, not a solution. But I knew that a gesture often spelled the difference between giving up on life or going on.

For several weeks I continued to make daily visits to the encampments. New friends began to wave at me as I pedaled by: Willie, Eunice, Peter, Old Nosepeg, Kaapa, Winnie, Left Hand Jim, and Louie Paga. I joined them whenever I could, mostly at their stone piles, where they stared off into space or looked down at the ground for hours at a time. During these long silent vigils they waited for something that never seemed to come and seemed to hope for something to take away their struggle and pain. Old men held my hands and cooed, their long slender fingers folding over mine in unspoken trust.

The Aborigines were dying a slow, horrifying death. Their nomadic ways, their art, dance, music, and oral history, which stretched back to the last ice age—all they possessed—had slipped through their hands like sand. They endured this collective death with quiet resignation. Perhaps this acquiescence stemmed from their belief that this life was a mere shadow of the real world, that beyond it lay the greater reality.

My association with the Aborigines was not unnoticed by the whites of Alice Springs. The police gave me a warning one afternoon when I tried to help an Aborigine woman they called Crazy Mary, a tall gangly lady with a misshapen head. I had found her running stark naked in heavy traffic. I got off my bike and pulled her to the side of the road where I sat her down and gave her water from my canteen. She looked hungry and pained. There was a wild expression in her eyes, and her thin face was contorted with fear. I told her to wait while I

Louie Paga

went to town to buy her a dress. (The women at the department store laughed when I told them what I was doing.) When I returned, the police were taking Mary off in a padded squad car. She was huddled—lonely, naked, and trembling—in a caged back seat. The officer stuck his finger in my chest and told me to mind my own business and to stop trying to help the Aborigines.

On another occasion, while making sandwiches for an Aborigine grandmother and her two small granddaughters in an alley outside a grocery store, a mud-spattered pickup truck came barrelling toward us. Two ranchers in T-shirts and blue jeans got out and yelled at me to get off private property. The woman and the small girls seemed unaffected by the men's anger and hatred, but I found their assault devastating. It left me feeling weak and nauseous. I continued to visit with the Aborigines as I had for the last ten days, but inside I felt overwhelmed by this calamitous cruelty toward fellow human beings. I was burning out.

I decided to leave. The day after the incident with the two ranchers, I made a last round of visits to the encampments to say good-bye to friends. They did not seem to understand my leaving any more than they had understood my coming. Many offered me their hands, loose fingers barely holding on to mine. It was an unspoken good-bye between people who had shared a little time and space on a pile of rocks. One old man touched the side of my cheek with the back of his hand and smiled.

On a steamy morning in early February I checked out of the YMCA, thanked Petra and Peter for their friendship and the use of their bike, and boarded a train called The Ghan, a turn-of-the-century relic that limped southward through the desert at twenty miles per hour. As the train pulled out of the station, I saw a handful of Aborigines sitting around the Howling Dingo Monument. I recognized Jim and Nosepeg and Kaapa and a few others. I felt my heart beating faster. I waved and turned my head to see them one last time, but they were oblivious to the train, and I went unnoticed. For the next few hours I sat morosely as the desert rolled by the window.

My seatmate got on a few hours later, a large raw-boned farmer with overalls and a slouched hat and clodhopper boots. He introduced himself as Jed and proceeded to tell me his life story. I stole away to the club car and drank with some Aussie travelers around an upright

Summer clouds, Orroroo

piano. A plump housewife in a print dress belted out old favorites. The train chugged through the desert, and the full moon bathed the sloping dunes in an eerie blue light. In between verses of "Waltzing Matilda," I pressed my face against the window and caught glimpses of kangaroos and dingoes, often at distances of no more than twenty yards. Some of the animals cavorted in the moonlight. One wise-looking kangaroo with a half smile on its face stared back at me. It was as if it knew who I was, and I saw in those soft eyes and face a good and caring soul. Returning to the singing and drinking I felt a sense of loss. Human beings know so little about their animal brothers and sisters.

A day later The Ghan pulled into Adelaide Station on the south coast. I disembarked and said good-bye to my seatmate, shouldered my rucksack, and began to hitch out of town. A "truckee" and his wife picked me up on the outskirts of town, and we headed north into the country's interior. It was broad, flat, wheat country, where the towns had names like Commeroo, Booleroo, Terowie, and Waylaya.

When we came to a small farming community called Orroroo, I got out. Orroroo was typical of the wheat towns on the edge of the southern outback. It had a 1930s feeling about it. Women in printed housedresses and sunbonnets shopped along the main street with wicker baskets on their arms. Farm men, dusty-faced and smiling, drove through town during the day in trucks loaded down with golden wheat. Orroroo caught my fancy and I stayed a couple of weeks, taking a room at the Commercial Hotel and renting a motorcycle from the local garage.

The owner of the Commercial Hotel, Peter Degman, took a special interest in seeing to my needs. He was a gregarious fellow who introduced me to the regular customers in his pub. They were farmers and ranchers who came into town for a game of darts and a pitcher of beer. One old regular, a grain mill operator by the name of Wilton Cox, took it upon himself to act as my "agent" for all local affairs. Wilton took me home the first night to meet the "Missus" and his family. We shared a boiled dinner of corned beef and cabbage, and when the stars came out he walked me home and taught me the constellations of the Southern Hemisphere: the Seven Sisters, Alpha Centauri, and the Southern Cross.

Miss Lucy and Miss Harriet penning cattle

Wilton was a great source of information. If he did not know the answer to my questions, he found out. When we drank at the pub, he often leaned back on his bar stool and called down to ask a friend a question. "Say Mort, is old man Braylard still ranching out in Terowie?" With Wilton's help I was able to make contact with a number of "local identities" (as old-timers there were called): the Shackleford brothers, who still plowed their wheat with an eight-horse hitch; Mr. A. I. MacAllum in Morchard, who took me to sheep and cattle auctions; and a sheep shearer and bounty rider by the name of Roy Baker, who knew how to predict the weather by the shape of the new moon.

But of all the local people I met, I liked the two Shephard sisters the best. Miss Lucy, seventy-one, and Miss Harriet, seventy, were single women ranching on their father's old cattle station out at Euralia. The Shephard sisters wore smocks and sunbonnets, muslin stockings with holes in them, and hightop basketball sneakers, and they often carried shepherd's canes. They were wisps, genteel women with British accents. They ranched alone on thousands of acres in the outback, without electricity, telephone, or automobile, much the way their parents had. Their one modern convenience was a tiny three-wheeled motorcycle which permitted them, when rheumatism was kicking up in their knees, to go two or three miles into the outback to bring their cattle in to drink at the water tanks.

My favorite time to visit with Miss Lucy and Miss Harriet was in the late afternoon when they trudged out into the hills to find their cattle. It was my job to open and close the final gate, a job that gave me time to lie on the warm red earth and watch the rosy-breasted parrots and gallahs bathing in the mossy water tubs. Soon I heard the sisters' hoots and hollers and the yelping of their thirteen red kelpie dogs, and saw a great procession of bellowing cattle driven forward by the two women, clouds of red dust billowing above them.

When the cattle had been penned for the night, they took me home for high tea. I always brought along a bag of fresh fruit from a market in Orroroo, and even though they knew I had it, they pretended it was a surprise. "Oh my, oh my, it's fruit again. How dear, how splendid of you to be so kind."

Over tea and scones heated on their wood-burning stove, Miss Lucy, Miss Harriet, and I sat in the parlor and made proper conversation. We talked mostly about the weather and the ongoing drought, *Orroroo and Down Under* 117

but some, too, about their coming-of-age in the desert outback. They spoke with quaint accents, interrupting each other to interject something the other had left out. They told me how they had walked to school as girls, a distance of six miles, and how their father had taught them to harness the eight-horse hitch for the huge wheat wagons their family drove down to the weekly market in Euralia (ten miles each way).

When it was time to go, the sisters walked me out to my motorcycle at the end of the long driveway, their thirteen kelpie dogs trotting obediently behind. We said a proper good-bye, a handshake and a few well-chosen words, and they urged me to come back as soon as I could. When I reached the top of the hill, I looked back in my rearview mirror and saw them standing in the low swale, waving white handkerchiefs in the dusk.

Sometimes after leaving the Shephards, I drove my motorcycle far out into the desert—twenty, forty, fifty miles and more—as far as I dared on a tankful of gas in the lingering light. I would turn off the key and slowly coast to a stop with the wind whistling through my hair and the tires hissing on the dry earth. Then silence. This was the way the desert had been since the beginning of time. I sprawled out on the still-warm sands and gazed up at the night skies turning from pink to violet to gray. If I lay still long enough, I would see a family of dingoes playing or a mob of kangaroos on their way to a watering hole.

There was something special about that dried-up red desert. It pulled at me like a magnet. Alone under the big sky, a brown lizard at my feet, vultures silhouetted in flight, the mountains shimmering in the lingering light, I imagined I was a traveler from outer space who had just come to earth. When the stars began to appear in the eastern sky, I got on my motorcycle and rode back into town. The hot air spilled over my naked chest and shoulders, and tears streamed down my face, making the earth, sky, and new moon all blurred and ethereal. Finally, the beckoning lights of little Orroroo appeared on the mountainside. Ten minutes later I wheeled the motorcycle into the hotel garage, showered off the dust and heat and magic of the desert, and sat down in the dining room for a quiet supper at a white-linened table.

On a sunny morning in February, a few weeks after my arrival in Australia, I left Orroroo to catch my scheduled flight for Auckland, New Zealand.

Lothlorien Orchards Farm

On my first day in New Zealand I drove up the coastal highway in a rented car and stopped at an organic peach stand to buy some fruit. When I asked the young man selling fruit if there were any traditional farmers about, he thought for a moment, and then said that where he lived people were farming in old ways. He was outgoing and friendly and invited me home with him. I stayed a month.

My friend lived on Lothlorien Orchards Farm, a land trust where a group of twelve adults and thirteen children farmed a hundred-acre parcel of rolling, up-island land. The people at the farm lived in small hand-hewn houses nestled in clumps of eucalyptus trees. The land trust had been started ten years earlier by a young couple from Detroit, Dale and Sharon, who still lived there with their three children. The farm—two thousand trees in all—grew vast quantities of organic, hand-picked peaches, nectarines, and grapefruits. Everyone owned a portion of the land trust, and in turn, the sale of the fruit took care of people's living expenses. It was a low-cost way for individuals to own and farm large tracts of land.

I pitched my tent in the orchards along the south edge of the property. My nearest neighbor was a New Zealander by the name of Trish, a lithe, pretty woman with long brown hair who lived in a small cabin with her one-year-old son Chinoo. Trish had built her own cabin with hand tools and had furnished it simply and beautifully: a white canopy bed, a blue enamel cookstove, print curtains, a rocking chair, and a wooden table. Her personal effects were few but meaningful: hawk feathers, blue shells, glazed pieces of rose pottery. I liked visiting with her. On soft summer nights we sat outside on the porch and watched fireflies sparkle in the tall grasses, and by candlelight we gently rubbed each other's feet.

During the harvest season, when the fruit lay heavy on the limbs, everyone picked together in the orchards. There was a festive feeling in the air. Families trundled down in the warm sunshine with boxes, crates, and ladders, and children and dogs frollicked nearby. Almost everyone went. A few preferred picking as a couple, like New Zealanders Stephen and Diane with their small baby Gabriel squirreled away in a backpack. Others picked at a slightly faster pace, like Tony, the hearty round-the-world traveler who had stopped off for a week and had stayed a year; Jo Bradshaw, a short, tan Australian woman who

Opal and Linden, sister and brother

had been at the farm for six years; and Andriano, the happy-go-lucky Italian who lived in the pottery shed above the barn.

By the end of the day there were mounds of ripe juicy fruit, fifty boxes or more. We gathered on the grass, tired, happy, and sticky, and ate to our hearts' content. The red juice from sweet peaches ran down our chins as we laughed. It was sweet labor: friends working together harvesting a crop they nurtured throughout the year. The shared work made the farm strong and cohesive. There was a power and a beauty in their way of life.

Noontime meals at the farm were usually communal affairs that rotated between the different households. Families walked down through the fields of waist-high grass, carrying covered dishes they had prepared on their wood-burning stoves. There were savory soups, brown rice, red and green vegatables, freshly baked whole grain breads, huge salads in wooden bowls with nasturtiums in the center, blackberry cobblers, peach pies with fresh whipped cream, and always a jug or two of sweet peach juice that we drank as others might water.

The children at the farm were high-spirited and happy youngsters who thrived in the atmosphere of shared work and play. They attended a red one-room schoolhouse in Ahuroa. Early in the morning, when the dew was heavy on the grass and the sun streamed through the pines, the children assembled at Jo Bradshaw's house for breakfast. Jo was an early riser who was happy to cook them oatmeal, scones and muffins with honey, jam, and sweet butter. They dawdled as long as they could until Jo chased them off. As often as not, the children rode their horses to school, down a trail through the woods, two and three bareback on each horse. I used to watch them as they went, a gaggle of uncombed, smudgy-faced kids bound for learning.

In the late afternoon, when the sun was hot and the air thick with dust and locust song, the children raced home from school, tore off their clothes, and ran to a pond near Dale and Sharon's house. There was an old dock in the middle, and the children swam out and lazed there naked, like small brown seals. Someone initiated a game of water tag, and they chased each other through the warm and cool currents of the pond, shrieking as they went. An old goose lived at the pond and joined in the games. So did the two farm dogs, Ollie and the pup, both nonswimmers who ran around the shores barking wildly.

Orroroo and Down Under 123

Jo Bradshaw and her daughters

I often took my supper with an older couple who lived in a school bus in a thicket of ponga trees down by the creek. Gordon and Beatrice and their two children were inveterate travelers committed to an alternative lifestyle. Gordon's face reminded me of many old-world faces I had seen in travel books: an Ethiopian herder, an Asiatic fisherman, an old Zen monk. He sat beside his campfire in baggy shorts, bare-chested, the sinewy veins in his strong arms bulging. Beatrice went barefoot and wore a three-quarter length skirt. Her long brown hair was pulled back, revealing a strong and sensitive face with a beatific smile. We roasted potatoes in the coals and drank homemade wine from old green bottles. Sitting around the fire we talked late into the night while the wind raced in the trees overhead. It seemed important and somehow fitting that Gordon and Beatrice had a fire on the ground every night.

Perhaps the person at the farm I spent the most time with was Jo Bradshaw, the Australian who lived in a big house with her three children, Joanne, 11; Vanessa ,9; and Nash, 8. She was a small, muscular woman with a shock of thick curly hair and a warm smile. Jo was probably the hardest working member of the land trust. No one, not even Dale who had started the farm ten years before, could keep up with her when she picked fruit.

She had a wonderful getaway spot, a tiny space in the back of the pottery shed in the barn. We liked to slip off there at night after the children had been read to and tucked into bed. We sat for long periods in silence, sipping wine or smoking grass, writing in our journals, or reading aloud to one another from a spiritual book called *Das Energy*. After a long day of harvesting fruit, we held each other, our muscles sore and bruised, our shirts off, our bare skin touching, warm and sticky from the fruit. Our hair was tousled and sweet-smelling from the blossoms in the trees. We listened to Phil Collins albums on the record player and drifted in and out of sleep. Candles and incense burned down to nothing, and the night crept in with its soft blackness, its whirring sleep.

Sometimes in the late afternoon, when the summer sun along the narrow dusty roads made the toi toi plants look feathery and surreal, I walked a mile down to Percy Tohloph's little farm to help with milking. Percy was a Bohemian farmer who still spoke in his native German. He and the other Bohemians in the valley often gathered at the pub in

Puhoi to make oompa-pa music on brass instruments, and to drink beer, smoke, and swap stories. They were the grandchildren of those who had immigrated from western Czechoslovakia in the 1860s as pioneers, brave men who had come with little more than an ax and a tent.

I came often to Percy Tohloph's farm to help bring his nine brindled cows down from the high slopes. Percy was a rugged, handsome man who always wore tall rubber boots and puffy trousers and a rainbow-colored wool beret the women at the farm had knitted for him. He walked with a swagger and a tilt, his muscular body lumbering from side to side.

The farm people adored old Percy Tohloph, and also another old bachelor down the road by the name of Roy Parker. Both men had a soft spot in their hearts for the folks at Lothlorien Orchards. Perhaps the men knew what work and determination it took to make a go of farming; perhaps the farm people served as an extended family. Regardless, the old men and the young people got on well together. Whenever someone needed a load of manure or a ditch dug with a backhoe, Percy or Roy would be there at a moment's notice. Money never changed hands; both groups preferred the old system of barter. The farm people reciprocated by cooking the bachelors a special dinner of roast chicken and gravy and garden vegetables, with a blackberry pie and fresh whipped cream for dessert. The men lingered after the meal with their coffee and a smoke. In the lamplight, with a child or two on their laps, they sat and talked for hours. When they were leaving, someone inevitably put a loaf of freshly baked bread under each man's arm.

One night we all piled into the 1947 Dodge truck and went to the movies in Warkworth. Sharon, Dale, and Tony sat up front in the cab, and nine of us stretched out on mattresses in the back, laughing and singing all the way into town. It was a beautiful summer night; the shadows were long and dark, and the air was soft on our skin. We drove slowly over the dirt roads from one valley into another, up steep grades and down. People waved as we went by: a farmer and his wife out inspecting their garden, a small boy running down from the hills with his young cows. We were a handsome sight, all tan and brown, strong-looking, laughing, with wheat chaff in our tousled hair and cowshit caked on our boots.

Roy Parker

Maori hunter, East Cape

When we arrived in Warkworth, I thought the townspeople would frown at us as we swaggered up the street, laughing, with bags of homemade popcorn under our arms and jugs of peach nectar in our hands. But they smiled and said hello. The farm people were known and respected for their honesty and hard work, and though a bit eccentric and colorful, they were well received in the community.

That night driving home from the movies there was a full moon. A mist hung in the lower valleys and in pockets along the hillsides. We rode home in silence most of the way, snuggled deep in mounds of blankets, our arms and legs entwined, and our heads resting on each other's shoulders. The moon sailed in the sky above us, appearing and disappearing in the clouds. Overhead the ponga trees were like fine gossamer lace, frilly against the moonlit sky. Someone hummed an old hymn and I found myself drifting in and out of sleep. Being in that old truck that night, with the moon in my eyes and the farm people lying close, was one of the happiest times of my life.

A few days later, after some sweet good-byes, I took leave of the Lothlorien people to continue my travels to the remote East Cape of North Island. I wanted to see the Maori people, the original New Zealanders. Driving south through a rain storm in a rented car, I knew that I was getting closer to the Maori villages when I began seeing hunters on fast horses crossing the road and heading up steep cliff trails. Coming around a bend in the road, I spotted a handsome man with shoulder-length hair who looked like Geronimo, a rifle slung over his shoulder, the carcass of a small decapitated deer draped over the horse's neck. Maori men, I had been told, were skilled hunters. The game they shot provided much of their families' food.

I stayed a week in a small lumbering town called Matahi, sleeping in my tent at night and hiking around the countryside during the day. Matahi sat at the end of a long steep valley three thousand feet high in the rain forest. Its dirt streets and houses on stilts reminded me of southern Appalachia. My tent was near the village school, and the first Maoris I came to know were the school children, happy youngsters with a singsong way of speaking. They called me John and often invited me to join them at recess to play warrior games in which we ran through the woods shrieking and hooting and chasing one another.

While staying at Matahi, two small children befriended me, an eleven-year-old girl by the name of Waimiringi, and her eight-year-old brother, Moi. They lived with their grandfather down the creek about a mile. Often after school the children stopped at my tent and asked me to walk home with them on a trail through the woods. We dawdled along the way to nap in clumps of sweet-scented ferns, and swam in deep pools at the base of the cliffs. Their small brown bodies slipped through the currents with ease.

The children's grandfather, a leathery-faced Maori with a long white beard and a woolly head of hair, waited for our return. His name was Nino Tacao and he lived in a small cabin by the creek. He plowed his garden with an old white horse and put up fruits and vegetables for the winter. He hunted on mountain slopes nearby, following trails that had been made by his people a thousand years ago. Deer, possum, wild pigs and goats, game birds, and rodents were his staples. Great green eels, however, were his delicacy, and on moonlit nights when the mist floated above the stream, Nino took me by torchlight to wander barefoot in pools where we netted the five-foot-long slimy creatures.

Old Nino and I enjoyed talking in the late afternoon when the children were doing their chores, chopping wood and hauling water. We sat under a tree and drank lemonade and ate salt biscuits, with the hunting dogs resting at our feet. He was typical of the old Maoris who kept alive the history of their people by telling stories that stretched all the way back to the journey of the "Seven Canoes" that sailed across the "Big Water" from Polynesia thousands of years ago. He pointed a gnarled old hand to the mountains and told me that it was there he felt most at home. When I asked him what he did in the mountains, he said he liked to take a handful of his grandchildren there to spend a week or more with only a rifle and a box of matches. He smiled as he told me how he and the young ones slept at night, curled up at the base of a giant tree in a huge pile of leaves, like a family of possums.

I lived in another village while visiting with the Maori, a rough-and-tumble mountain logging town called Ruatahuna. Horses and colts roamed freely here, goats and fat pigs drank at mud puddles, and gaudy white and gold chickens roosted in every available tree. While in Ruatahuna I camped out near the barn of a young shepherd, a soft-spoken, kind-eyed man by the name of Manu Tepou. The first time I saw Manu, he was standing in the rain at dusk, shoeing his horse. The orange light from his forge fell across his gentle features as he looked up from his work and welcomed me. He told me he was heading off in the early morning to bring down three wild bulls and asked if I wanted to come along.

Manu and I left the village the following morning at dawn. The unlit houses and barns looked like phantoms in the gray drizzle. Six cattle dogs trotted beside us, black skinny animals with red tongues that lolled from side to side in their mouths. We rode up through forests of eucalyptus and pine, great stands as tall and straight as schooner masts. Manu was a beautiful horseman who rode with a western saddle and guided his horse with gentle fingers and a light touch of his legs. Like any good horseman, he was able to open and close cattle gates without getting on and off his mount.

In the eerie light we came upon the bulls: brutish monsters, thick-necked and mean. My horse sensed my fear and moved cautiously to the side. Manu removed his whip and swung it around his head a half-dozen times. It hissed as it sliced up through the soft, rain-filled air. *Crack!* The bulls moved down to the right, and the dogs moved in lashing out at their hind legs. The bulls were herded down to the lower valley where Manu and his brother coralled them in sturdy pens.

It was easy to meet the Maori people. Tourists were few and far between and everywhere I went someone seemed eager to invite me to his home. One afternoon a jolly, bare-chested man with no teeth and loose trousers found me wandering in the hills behind the village. His name was Manuhi, and he was a Maori bushman, or logger, who had been laid off from the mill and now walked many hours in the forests for exercise. He was friendly and insisted I come back to his little cabin, a bachelor's nest that was spare and rustic. His skinny hound lay in the corner thumping his tail on the floorboards, and two brown hens slep on the counter by the hand pump. He made me a delicious tea from herbs he had gathered in the hills, and he sweetened it with honey from his hives. We talked for nearly an hour, his big-knuckled hands almost touching mine on the table top, and I sensed his yearning for a visitor to listen to his stories.

After our visit Manuhi took me next door to meet his auntie, a Polynesian woman in her late sixties. She stood in the doorway of her cabin smoking a pipe, staring off toward the mountains. She was a jolly woman: thin, toothless, and animated. Her arms waved about as she spoke. After a short period of porch talk, she took me in to see her house. It was as if she was showing me the Taj Mahal. Of particular interest to her, and therefore to me, was a wall of photographs, including pictures of her mother and father, her uncles in military uniforms somewhere in the South Pacific, a color print of Mother Mary, and one of Christ ascending to heaven. There was an oval-framed photograph of Queen Elizabeth and Prince Phillip, and a picture that my host deemed particularly extraordinary: a shot of the Queen Mother in a grass skirt officiating at a Maori Festival.

A wedding took place while I was in Ruatahuna, and through the two nieces of the bride, little sisters by the name of Pae Teka and Peho, I was invited to the community banquet at the local marae. Maraes were places of worship for the Maori people, small wooden buildings with carved totems on the roof depicting myths, gods, and demons.

People began arriving in the early afternoon. Some arrived in old funky cars, giant gas-guzzling, chrome-plated barges with eight or ten Maoris stuffed inside, laughing and carrying on. Other guests arrived on horseback: small wiry men with thin mustaches in ill-fitting black suits and large comely women in flowery dresses riding sidesaddle, each with a flower behind her ear. The marae was filled with bright bouquets and garlands of orchids. There was music from guitars and drums, and small children promenaded up and down the hall with their arms about each other's waists. Outside, bare-chested men as huge as sumo wrestlers cooked whole pigs and sides of beef, chicken, possum, deer, goat, and wild turkey on hissing grates laid over open pits. Voluminous women with creamy, chocolate skin moved about the hall with enormous platters of steaming yams and sweating potatoes, bowls of soft mushy corn, steamed greens, squash, and turnips, and a gooey, stinky corn dessert that had fermented for five months, which everyone seemed anxious to devour.

The minister, a thin woolly-headed man in a black cloth shirt, who wore gold-rimmed spectacles, said the blessing as everyone gathered around the bride and groom. Soon people began loading their plates at the serving table—not just one helping, but two, three, and four heaping platefuls of the delicious food—all the while laughing and carrying on. The father of the bride, a natty gentleman in a white suit and a flowered tie, made his way slowly about the hall, grinning and kissing people, who seemed annoyed to have to wipe their mouths and leave their food to return his kiss.

I visited with the school children whenever I could, and welcomed the opportunity to speak to them as a group. Often the teacher or the principal asked me to say a few words about my own family and village back in New England, and to share some of my travel experiences. I especially enjoyed telling the children about our winters. I told them how the snows came so hard that sometimes the drifts would be over my head, and that the ice on the ponds got thick enough for a truck to drive over them safely. They gasped and held their hands over their mouths in disbelief.

The children also shared their history and told stories from their own mountain villages. In particular they told me about a local hero named Rua the Prophet, a nineteenth-century Maori leader who dreamt of uniting New Zealand's Polynesian people. Rua had made a long pilgrimage deep into the forest with his followers, had established a capital there, and was well on his way to creating a separate Maori state when he died. Ruatahuna was one of the nine Maori villages Rua had founded.

When the children asked me about my heroes, I told them stories about Martin Luther King Jr., Abraham Lincoln, John F. Kennedy, and Jackie Robinson. I also told them about less well-known heroes like Rosa Parks, who had refused to give up her bus seat to a white man, and in so doing had helped launch the civil rights movement.

The Maori children often responded to my talks by sharing some of their thoughts and feelings about peace. They explained there was a movement afoot in New Zealand that encouraged Maoris to return to their roots, to come home to the land that once had taken care of them. The children told me how older brothers and sisters, uncles and aunts, cousins, and even grandparents were leaving the bigger cities like Auckland to re-establish traditional villages in the mountains, where many of the old ways remained. I told the children about the people at Lothlorien Orchards Farm and how some *pakeha* (white people) were also returning to a simple, more satisfying way of life.

Driving down from Ruatahuna to Auckland's international airport, I was filled with melancholy. My new-found Maori friends and I had exchanged photos and promises to write, but in our hearts we knew we would probably not see each other again. After nearly three months "down under," I was heading home to Connecticut, a place so far away no one here had heard of it.

Summer encampments, Whale Cove

WHALE COVE

July 3, 1983. LaGuardia Airport. I ate my breakfast in one of those strange fast-food alcoves: white toast and coffee and scrambled eggs. Above me on the wall loomed a giant photograph of Mayor Fiorello LaGuardia reading the funnies over the radio during the 1945 newspaper strike. As I walked out of the restaurant with my sheepskin vest and knapsack over my shoulder, a redcap stood near the doorway and looked quizzically at my attire. "Where you going, boy?" I told him that I was on my way up to the North Pole to visit the Eskimos. He rolled his eyes and said, "Whew-eee."

At the Minneapolis/St. Paul Airport my connecting flight to Winnipeg was delayed an hour, so I sat and practiced looking at fellow travelers without judging them. There were businessmen smoking cigarettes and rich women wearing endangered-species furs; backpackers with long hair and inner city youths carrying "ghetto blasters"; farmers, ranchers, northerners, southerners, rich, poor, black, white, red, yellow. Unsuccessful, I gave up after half an hour or so.

I landed in Winnepeg that afternoon. From Winnipeg I planned to take a train north to Churchill on the shores of Hudson Bay. From Churchill I would travel to one of the Innuit villages, but I did not know which one. As I made my way into the main lobby, fifty or more musicians were gathered in small groups. Passersby came close to catch an earful of the music before boarding their planes. I asked one of the musicians, a young woman in a prairie skirt who carried a Celtic drum, what the gathering was all about. She told me musicians from all over North and South America had come to Winnipeg for the Winnipeg Folk Festival. She said that if I went, I would not be sorry.

I rescheduled my trip, and spent the next four days at the Winnipeg Folk Festival, with the train ticket for my journey in the back hip pocket of my blue jeans. Festival-goers camped in the prairies on the

outskirts of the city to listen to Taj Mahal, Leo Kottke, Queen Ida, Loudon Wainwright III, and four hundred other performers. There was Cajun music and bluegrass, boogie-woogie and soul, French Canadian and Maritime, Delta blues, Chicago blues, southern gospel, Andean Indian, native American, and just plain American folk music. The highlight of the four days was Vassar Clements playing "The Orange Blossom Special" on his fiddle. Forty thousand people rose to their feet and stomped as a huge red sun dropped beneath the Manitoba prairie.

On July 8th, as the late afternoon sunlight streamed through the railway station windows, I boarded a Canadian Pacific train in Winnipeg for the north country. My seatmates were two Crees—trappers, I thought—a husband in a wool mackinaw and a wife in a flowered skirt and parka. They were eating cheap blue ice cream from small dixie cups when I sat down, their gnarled old hands having trouble with the tiny wooden spoons. They whispered to one another in their language, and occasionally looked up at me with soft brown eyes.

The train took two full days to wind its way from Winnipeg to Churchill. The first leg of the journey crossed the wheat fields of southern Manitoba: mile after mile of rolling fertile green prairies, green with hay shimmering in the last light of the summer sun. From time to time I went out and stood between the swaying cars. Leaning out of the open doorway I watched small villages flash by. Boys on bicycles waited at the crossroads with their dogs and waved.

At Dauphin, where the great prairies began to give way to the spruce and pine forests of the north, our train stopped to take on water. I walked out into the dusk to stretch my legs in a nearby park and came upon a solitary man sitting on a bench, a farmer in a dark woolen suit and boots who seemed open to conversation. He greeted me in a thick accent, and when I asked him if he was French, he said no, he was a Ukranian. Then he pointed his hand to the northwest to remind me where Russia was. The whistle of the train blew, the conductor leaned out and yelled "all aboard" and I was forced to leave my Ukranian friend behind without ever finding out what had made him decide to come to Dauphin.

When I took my seat again, the Crees had gone—for a hunting camp, perhaps, somewhere deep in the forest along the tracks. In their place sat two men, rough-hewn farmers in their seventies, with baggy trousers and short-sleeved shirts, holding Bibles in their hands. They introduced themselves as Mr. Henry Brown and Mr. Raymond Henry, both from Riding Mountain, Manitoba. They told me they were on their way to Churchill to see the sights and to "witness" to those in need who had not found their salvation. They were Jehovah's Witnesses.

Right from the start I liked these men immensely. They were both what good travelers should be: excited about what they had never seen before. Even in the dark, as the train barrelled through the invisible Canadian forest, they sat at the very edge of their seats savoring their journey.

The men were frugal travelers. They had brought brown paper bags of food—smoked sausages and brown bread—and a thermos of coffee that we all shared. We talked late into the night until we noticed our light was the last one to be extinguished. We turned in and slept as well as anyone ever sleeps on trains, half aware of the strange-sounding names of towns shouted out in the night by the conductor, lulled by the swaying of the train and the clickety-clack of the rails.

In the morning I awoke to find Mr. Brown and Mr. Henry resuming their vigil on the edge of their seats. The train continued on through the forests, enveloped in a cold drizzle. If the foul weather and the gloomy forests dampened my spirits, they had a reverse affect on the old gentlemen, sparking them to regale me with stories of their own adventures in northern Saskatchewan and the Yukon. Mr. Brown began telling Robert Service stories about the north country, and even gave a rousing rendition of "The Cremation of Sam McGee."

On the second day toward dusk the land began to change. Large pine and spruce gave way to dwarf species that later gave way to shrubs and bushes. Finally the treeless landscape of the tundra appeared. Somewhere in the middle of the night the rain abated, the fog lifted, and the full moon appeared. Everyone on the train was asleep except for me and Mr. Brown and Mr. Henry. We sat looking out in silence at the eerie landscape: a rolling tundra of scoured stone and moss that swept a thousand miles to the north, unimpeded by even a single tree.

On the morning of the third day we reached Churchill, the end of the line. The temperature at the railway station stood at thirty-six degrees, and a cold wind blew off the ice on Hudson Bay through the

Author camped out on outskirts of Churchill

treeless town. I shouldered my backpack and said good-bye to my two traveling friends, wished them luck and adventure, and promised that someday I would look them up.

Churchill was a small shipping port on the western shore of Hudson Bay. Grain trains came up through the southern prairies of Saskatchewan and Manitoba to ship wheat to Europe and Russia. It was a frontier town of about five thousand souls who braved the long winters. A few cars and trucks wound up and down the main street, and a handful of tourist buses circumnavigated the town, with passengers eagerly looking for polar bears. A Russian freighter lay in port waiting for the ice to go out.

I spent four days in Churchill numbed to the bone, even when wearing all the clothes I had brought (seven layers). The town was locked in with fog. I was forced to wait for the weather to break before I could catch a flight north to Whale Cove, an Innuit village. With time on my hands, I camped at the edge of town near a string of log cabins and shacks that belonged to Cree Indians. These were hardscrabble neighborhoods, with worn pathways strewn with whiskey bottles and beer cans, the skins of seals, bears, and caribou. There were a handful of Eskimo sled dogs tethered on stout chains who slept like sprawling lions on the roofs of their houses. They raised mournful howls as I passed on the way to my tent.

One of the Crees, a kind man by the name of Charlie Fox, allowed me to camp by his house. He warned me that a large polar bear had been prowling about for the last week and told me to be cautious. Charlie came out five or six times during the day, and sometimes at night, to make sure I was all right. I thought the bear was just an excuse to talk, but when he made a booby trap out of bells, tin cans, rope, and wire, I believed him.

Finally the weather broke and the temperature shot all the way up to forty-five degrees. I booked a flight on Calm Airways to Whale Cove, two hours to the north. A whaling and fishing village of two hundred Innuits, Whale Cove had been recommended to me by a Catholic priest who had spent forty years collecting Innuit artifacts for the mission museum in Churchill. While waiting in the small airport, I lay up against my backpack on the floor and watched a group of Innuits also waiting for the flight. It was my first good look at the people I hoped to visit. They were an extremely jolly bunch: toothless grandmothers laughing; young mothers sitting with fat smiling babies; fishermen and hunters in rubber boots and T-shirts smoking cigarettes; and small boys and girls playing cat's cradle on the floor. Their eyes were dark and almond-shaped and they had soft round faces. All of them spoke Innuit, a beautifully resonant clicking language, and their hands and arms would suddenly fly out with explosive exclamations. They were not at all self-conscious and lay on the floor as if they were in their own living rooms. They even managed to pull me into their conversation, asking me where I was going. When I told them Whale Cove, one fat old hunter in a white T-shirt and boots did a funny pantomime, shivering with his arms about his waist, as if to say "Ole Whitey gonna freeze his ass off," and everyone laughed.

In the late afternoon we boarded the plane, a small two-engine craft that held about twenty passengers. We circled the field several times and then catapulted off to the north over Churchill, the last link with the modern world. We flew low over the land and sea, three thousand feet and lower, straddling the western shoreline. The late afternoon sun was partially obscured by intermittent rain clouds, but it broke through from time to time, bathing the lands below in bronze. Muskeg barrens of sphagnum moss and sedge grass rolled gently to the west, and ground vapors swallowed whole quadrangles of the land. Rivers flowed eastward from a thousand nameless lakes. Brown beaches of mud and slime spread along the shoreline. Hudson Bay was locked in tight, and the pack ice and icebergs extended as far as Quebec Province, 450 miles to the east.

For nearly two hours the plane's small engines droned as we drifted over this strange and wonderful country. I had never seen land like this before, and I wondered what it must have been like for the Innuits who, until a mere thirty years ago, had lived there as nomads for thousands of years. Finally I spied a small settlement on the horizon. Two Innuits on the other side of the aisle reached out and tugged at my pant leg. They made funny signs, shivering as they told me that the village out there was Whale Cove. The plane's motors whined, and we descended to a small dirt runway on a spit of land that jutted into the sea. As the plane's tires touched down, crates, boxes, and babies bounced high in the air. The Innuits laughed and joked and made hand signs indicating the plane was blowing up. When we came to a stop, the pilot lowered the stairs, handed me my backpack, and wished me well, saying that he would be back in three weeks. I looked down the runway. Not a single person or vehicle. Just swirling dust and stony cobble and the pack ice on the horizon. Timidly I placed one foot on the stairs, then turned back and looked at the Innuits, whose smiles and dancing eyes encouraged me. My dream of living with the Innuits was coming true.

I stood and watched the plane taxi down the runway, rev its engines, and take off. If Churchill had been cold, then Whale Cove in the Northwest Territories was downright frigid. The wind blew unmercifully off the ice, and managed to sneak into all the interstices of my clothing. For ten minutes, alone and buffeted by the wind, I waited for something, for what I was not sure. Maybe the Connecticut Limousine Service, which had taken me home from LaGuardia so many times. Just when I could not take another minute of the cold, a pickup came barreling onto the runway and stopped at my feet. An Innuit man dressed in blue jeans and a white T-shirt jumped out cheerfully, took my bag and put it in back, and welcomed me. He said his name was Andy and that he was the taxi for Whale Cove.

On the way into town I asked Andy if he could please roll up his window. He laughed and obliged. He talked during the five-minute ride but I really could not concentrate on what he was saying. I was absorbed by the beauty of the soft light of dusk on the tundra. Just before Whale Cove Andy turned off the road, drove up onto a bluff that overlooked the bay, and stopped. He said I could put my tent there. We walked over to a lee in the cliff. Nearby, in a small seep hole in the rocks, he showed me where I could collect rainwater for drinking and bathing. He seemed happy to help me. I told him he reminded me of a friendly cab driver in New York City who might show a country person a good restaurant or an inexpensive hotel. He smiled.

Andy continued down the hill in his truck to the beach, where he parked and went inside a white tent. He returned on foot a few minutes later with a box of provisions. He had brought cans of sardines and stew, crackers and jam, tea and cocoa mix, and told me I would be warmer once I got some food in my belly. I thanked him, and then watched as he made his way back to his tent on the beach. In the fading light I cooked supper on my small Primus stove, brewed up some cocoa, and ate sitting down on some soft moss in a pile of rocks out of the wind. As I ate I watched some white seagulls fly across the pink and orange skies over the bay. Not long afterward I set up my tent. As I lay in my sleeping bag and watched a few lone stars appear in the south, I gave silent thanks for having arrived safely in the land of the Innuit.

I slept well that first night, dreaming of ice and snow, mud barrens and cold streams. In the morning I woke to find the wind and cold had been replaced by a soft drizzle that coated the landscape. I cooked some of Andy's cocoa, ate a handful of crackers, and then walked across the hill by my tent to take a look at the village that would be my home for the next three weeks.

Whale Cove sat on a peninsula that ran out into the sea. A group of about fifty weather-beaten government-built homes hugged the shoreline. It was Sunday morning and not a soul stirred. Sled dogs on chains got up stiffly to sniff at me as I walked past. One or two howled and then walked back to their dog houses to curl up and sleep.

My first impression of the village was not a good one. Litter and debris were everywhere: great mounds of garbage in plastic bags, rotting hides of animals, and caribou antlers. There were castaway parts of Evinrude outboards, Ski-Doo treads, the innards of three-wheel Hondas, junked motorcycles, old windows, discarded toasters, television sets with broken screens, dog bones, old mattresses, and a washing machine with oil cans stuffed inside. The town seemed sad and forlorn, especially in the cold, gray light. I challenged myself to hang tough and look for what was good, reminding myself that I had been to suburban towns in Westchester County where the lawns were immaculate and the houses neat and elegant, but a warm and happy smile almost impossible to find.

The priest in Churchill had given me the name of a married couple in Whale Cove, Mary and John Sigurdson. He thought they could assist me. Mary ran a small bakery, and her husband John, the only white person in the village, was a shipping clerk for the local airline. While looking for them I found a teenage boy tinkering with his motorcycle who directed me to a small shingled house at the end of a row of similar homes. When I knocked, a woman of about thirty with short-cropped hair appeared at the door. She greeted me and told me to come in. She introduced herself as Mary Sigurdson and then introduced me to her family: nine-year-old Christine, and three rough-and-tumble boys all under the age of six. John Sigurdson, a tall solemn man in his fifties,

Old Louisa and young Louisa with baby

shyly shook my hand and then went quickly back to the paperwork at his desk. Mary said John was always busy with his work.

Over coffee and sweet rolls in Mary's kitchen, I explained that I wanted to learn about traditional cultures, and that I hoped to meet some of the older residents of the village. She laughed and said hardly anyone ever came to Whale Cove, and while she was not quite sure what I wanted to see, we could start with her parents, who lived a few houses away.

As Mary and I walked along the shore to her parents' house, the frozen ice in the bay looked gray and forbidding. The dooryard of her parents' home was strewn with old machine parts and the skins of polar bears and caribou. The carcass of a freshly killed seal sat on the sagging front steps, its blood and guts oozing out. Mary laughed and said it looked like her brothers had been out hunting.

Inside the house Mary's parents, Louisa and Leo, both in their sixties, sat at a kitchen table working on a pair of sealskin (*mukluk*) boots. Mary spoke to them in Innuit, and they rose from the table, avoiding my eyes, embarassed perhaps, or uncomfortable greeting a white stranger. Louisa said something to me in Innuit which was almost inaudible, and Leo weakly offered me a limp right hand. Nearby, five of Mary's teenage brothers watched a baseball game on the television set, each wearing tight-fitting blue jeans and a T-shirt. Two of Mary's sisters were cooking bread in the kitchen and leaned out to welcome me in English. Louisa busied herself with fresh coffee as Leo offered me a cigarette. We smoked in silence until the women's return. And then for nearly two hours, with Mary serving as an interpreter, I questioned the old people about igloos, sled dogs, winter, trapping, hunting, and the long marches on the tundra in search of caribou. When I asked what year they had come to Whale Cove, Leo responded with a long story about the Keewatin Eskimo people. On the brink of starvation in the 1940s and 1950s, they were unable to live as nomadic hunters because of the dwindling number of game. In the early 1960s, the Canadian government relocated his people to Whale Cove to become whalers and fishermen. He made the long haul of 250 miles with his dogsled transporting Louisa and their four young children.

Louisa was a leathery-faced woman who looked as though she could still go through an arctic winter in an igloo. We talked and became more at ease with each other. Louisa showed me the *mukluk* boots she was making for Leo. To make them she had cured the skin of a seal one of her sons had killed. When I asked Louisa what type of thread she used, she went into the bedroom and returned with the bloody backbone of a caribou. She extracted the sinew to use as thread. Ten feet away the teenage sons cheered as Gary Carter hit a home run for the Montreal Expos. I sat there holding the caribou backbone, watching Louisa's and Leo's lined faces and intelligent eyes. They looked back at me as if they could read my mind. Would the younger generation ever remember the ways of their people?

Later that day Mary took me down to the family's summer camp—a few tents on the shore. When we got there, Louisa, Leo, and a handful of their children were at work in the cold rain pulling in long fish nets filled with arctic char. Leo seemed happy I had come. He grabbed a two-foot char from the nets and held it up for me to see, explaining in pidgin English that the fish were small this year, thin and scabby.

Mary discovered a giant red jellyfish in the nets and took time to observe its pulsing gelatinous matter, intricate veins, and yellow egg sacks. Seven or eight of the family gathered around and made low whispering sounds as they, too, found beauty in the sea creature.

When the family had removed ten or twelve of the ensnared char, they packed the fish in three wooden crates that they then dragged to a nearby tent. Louisa rummaged in a kindling box outside the tent for bunches of dried moss, and made a small fire on the ground. In this land of permafrost where no trees grew, sphagnum moss was the traditional fuel. Louisa watched as I stood about and then decided I should be offered the best caribou hide to sit on. One of her teenage sons, Peter, winked at me for the royal treatment I was getting. I winked back and smiled. Soon all the members of the family were at work outside the tent gutting the fish and preparing them for drying on long clotheslines near the tents. Dried arctic char was both a delicacy and a staple during the long winter months.

I started spending more time with Mary's family. Often in the evening the family gathered on the shore to restore the fishing boat *Ungava Queen*. The boat, a thirty-five foot trawler, had been a gift from the eleven children to their parents. Both of them had cancer—Leo, of the leg, and Louisa, of the ear. While there was still time, the children wanted to thank their parents for bringing them this far along.

Anticipating the ice going out, we worked extra hours to get the boat ready for its initial voyage. Each night we scraped and sanded the hull, replaced fittings on the rigging, and varnished the gunwhales and rudder. Then, on a warm evening, with the arctic sun still high in the sky at ten o'clock, we lifted the tall mast by stages into the mast hole and secured it with guy wires. Afterwards, Leo and I rested on the warm sand beach with a thermos of coffee and a couple of cigarettes, talking as best we could, mostly about his early days of sailing. When I asked him what kind of instrumentation guided him across the 450 miles of open water to Quebec Province, he laughed and told me that he navigated by the stars, and by the blood of his ancestors that coursed through his veins.

When not spending time with Mary's family, I enjoyed lying around in my tent. Below my camp on the shoreline the villagers' summer tents dotted the beach. During the day the village men chugged across the open stretches of water in their long motorized canoes in search of beluga whales. Others preferred hunting on the tundra for migratory bands of caribou. It was not uncommon to see a canoe filled with brothers returning at sunset with caribou haunches stacked in the hull.

I loved the view from my tent. Pack ice and humped ridges of icebergs stretched down the bay to the south and east. When the wind was out of the south, the ice moved north a bit and the bay opened up. Belugas came in to feed and play. In the dark blue water their white bodies looked luminous. Sometimes I saw as many as a hundred whales, their spouting interrupting the calm of the bay.

To the west the tundra stretched on with intermittent depressions, water-filled sloughs where geese,ducks, and gulls congregated. And while the landscape was not spectacular in a sensational way, the intricate orange and blue-green lichens that covered the smooth granite outcroppings lent a peculiar beauty to the scenery.

Each day I walked as far as I could on the tundra, past the little graveyard with its small wooden crosses, into the rolling esplanades of wheatgrass and moss where foxes and *sik-siks* (rodents) played. On the crests of the hills that overlooked the bay to the south, *inookshuks* —ancient stone cairns—marked good fishing spots that some Innuit had wanted to remember long ago. The arctic sky was sometimes huge and ominous-looking, but often the heavens were blue and serene. I

Playing on an ATV

loved tramping alone out on the tundra with a sandwich in my rucksack and a pair of binoculars to watch the small herds of caribou.

The children of Whale Cove often stopped at my tent to challenge me to a game of jacks on the flat rocks. I usually won. A game of their own, which I was not particularly good at, was scrambling over the ice. On warm July afternoons, when the arctic sun beat down on the rotting pack ice, leaping from berg to berg was scary business. The open patches of water were lovely, blue-green and clear, and far below the surface the ice had a turquoise glow. Little moon-faced brothers and sisters led me across the ice. Whenever we broke through, getting soaked to our knees, we shrieked and hooted. Hearing our laughter the elders could not contain themselves and rushed down from their houses to join in the fun. The old men and women, in pigtails and tall rubber boots, lept across the beach with joy.

On Sunday mornings I went to church with Mary and her family. We sat at the back of the small wooden Catholic mission: Louisa and her granddaughter, Mary, Christine, baby Denise, Peter, and I. Leo preferred to work on the *Ungava Queen*. I loved being in that simple white church by the sea. Old men and women, their arthritic legs in baggy woolen pants and moccasins, walked in halfway through the service. I watched the backs of their heads and wondered how many winters they had survived in an igloo on the barrens, and how many caribou they had shot. Many of the small children peeked from behind their mothers to look at the strange-looking *kabloona* (white).

On Sunday afternoons Mary's clan held a picnic at their tent down by the bay, an event to which I was always invited. Mary's daughter Christine usually picked me up on her three-wheeled Honda. I had to hug her about her waist to keep from falling off as we careened, shrieking and laughing, over stones and marshy esplanades. Other children were out on their machines as well, and quite often we came precariously close to colliding, an event that always brought them to laughter.

Sunday picnics were gatherings where the Innuits worked and played together. Almost twenty people gathered in the sunshine at Louisa and Leo's tents: old grandmothers in fur-lined parkas sitting with babies on their laps; "aunties" cooking caribou on small moss fires; men in rubber boots, T-shirts, and mirror sunglasses, smoking in a circle; and teenage boys and girls playing a rough-and-tumble baseball game with two bats. As most of the grown-ups spoke only Innuit, I usually played ball—to the delight of the children who enjoyed watching my inept play.

In the late afternoon Leo gave his bimonthly pep talk on how members of the family needed to pull their own weight to make the world a better place to live in, to make their family stronger, and to make their relationship with God more enduring. Mary whispered in my ear that her father had survived a tragic childhood. At birth his mother held him up by the leg and put him out on an iceberg because they were too poor to raise another child. Somehow someone saved him. But his life had been difficult. There had been little money for warm shoes, boots, or coats. And to make it all more devastating, he had watched his father take his own life.

When Leo had finished speaking, Joan, an eighty-year-old woman with a wrinkled face and eyes that twinkled stood up. She bent down and picked up a mussel shell and asked the family if they knew what it was. She then proceeded to explain that the shell had a function in life, and that each member of the family, too, had a purpose, a mission. The shell served as an introduction to a creation myth about how the animals and the ancient people had come to the land of ice and snow. The small children gazed up in wonder as she spoke.

A whale was killed during my stay, a small adult male beluga, about fifteen feet in length. One of my neighbors, who camped down by the cove, came up and told me about the kill and asked if I wanted to come along and see it. We walked down in a gray mist to the shore, where the two hunters who shot the whale had dragged it onto the beach. It bled bright red onto the smooth round pebbles, and the water was murky with blood. All that afternoon women in shawls, long skirts, and boots came down with baskets and their *ulu* knives to take their fair share of the kill back to their families. A few older couples came to collect oil from a gland in the whale's head for their moss-wick lamps. Three boys sat on the ground and peeled thin strips of the whale skin, which was considered a delicacy when eaten raw. Every part of the whale was used by the village. The blubber was fed to the tethered sled dogs who howled on the hillsides above the village.

That night, as the sun was setting on the bay, a neighbor, Solomon

Louisa and young friend

Voisey, came by to see if I wanted to share a meal of the whale meat with him and his wife. Solomon, like so many of the villagers, had a "service job." He helped run the village, and his wife Eva was the mayor of Whale Cove. At first I hesitated, not wanting to eat whale meat. But then I realized the Innuits hunted with reverence for the whales, and they had an intuitive respect for the balance of nature. I accepted his invitation.

We ate on the ground, the shortwave radio snarling and hissing out news about someone down at Eskimo Point who had hurt his leg. While Eva cooked *muktuk* (whale meat), Solomon and I sat with our feet stretched out in front of us, Innuit style, and talked. Eva served the *muktuk* with boiled potatoes, raw onions, catsup, white bread, and sweet black tea. They said an Innuit prayer for the whale, giving thanks for its life and for the sustenance it gave their people. Then we began to eat, picking up the meat with our fingers and licking them, our eyes lighting up at the taste. The *muktuk* had a delicious fishy taste. Solomon said it came from the vast quantities of fish on which the whale fed.

One afternoon while lazing in the sunshine outside my tent, Mary's eighteen-year-old younger sister, Monica, came by on her Honda three-wheeler and asked if I wanted to go for a picnic with Mary and some of the village children at a small lake out on the tundra. I accepted and we rode together on a small grassy road up along the coast. The lake lay about a mile to the north where the land peaked in small hills, creating long views. The arctic sun shone high in the sky even at 6 P.M., a honey-colored light that covered us with its glow.

Mary brought along a twenty-five-pound haunch of frozen caribou meat that she left on a flat stone with cakes, cookies, and sweet black tea. I watched the children cut off pieces of the raw red meat with the *ulu* knife and eat them with great relish as they darted off to play.

In early evening the children stripped down to their underwear and waded out into the cold clear pond to look for frogs' eggs and insects in the tall bullrushes. I too stripped down to my underwear and waded out to join in their games. It was a beautiful calm evening. A gentle wind stirred. Mosquitos and black flies buzzed slowly about us. Some of the children had removed their shirts, and in the yellowing light their brown skin reminded me of other native Americans I had known,

Boy with pups

far to the south in Arizona and New Mexico.

As the children and I inspected the intricate web of a yellow spider, Monica yelled out from the shore, "Hey, Kabloona, where d'ja get them white legs?" Her sisters, Mary and Gretta and little Louisa, giggled. When I came back to shore, Mary whispered to me that Monica had a crush on me and that she was looking for a white husband. Mary went on to explain that their old grandmother, who had died just a few years ago, had prophesied that many of the granddaughters would avoid a life of hardship and disaster if they married a *kabloona*—as Mary had done. Mary and I smiled and shrugged our shoulders.

While the children played at the pond, I stole away at sunset to wander alone in sloughs and muskeg bogs that reminded me of the moors of the Outer Hebrides. The light on the land was like autumn, and white sea gulls circled and screamed overhead in the blue sky. To the west an *okpik* (owl) hooted in the tall grasses. I lay down and rested in the moss, golden lichen at my head and feet, the dank smell of the warm earth pungent and yeasty. The children's cries and laughter were carried to me on the wind from just over the hill. And for a few brief minutes I lay circling, with nothing for reference but the sky and a swarm of mosquitoes above my head. I dreamt that I, too, was an Innuit and that this world of tundra and ice and water, and huge arctic sky had always been my home.

I asked Solomon Voisey how the Innuits said "good-bye." He said they did not have a word for "hello" or "good-bye." A big smile sufficed for both. Mary went on to elaborate: in the old days, when everyone lived in igloos, visitors on the barrens were infrequent and very special. After a week or so of visiting, the eventual parting was so difficult that they simply smiled and said something like, "We'll be seeing you again."

On a warm Sunday morning in late July, I smiled at Leo and Louisa on the tiny airstrip, hugged Mary and said: "I'll be seeing you."

Kaleniya Temple, outside Colombo

AMBEPUSSA

In the winter of 1984 I traveled from New York to Sri Lanka. I wanted to spend some time in a country whose government and people were predominantly Buddhist because I had become a student of Buddhism.

While driving in from the airport to Colombo, any preconceptions I had of a Buddhist country being superior were quickly laid to rest. Wherever I looked, I saw destruction and carnage: the burned homes and shops of the Tamil Hindu minority. My cab driver, himself a Tamil, explained in broken English that the violence had erupted during the summer, and the Sinhalese Buddhist majority had attacked the Tamils because of religious and racial differences. When I asked my driver whether he had been affected by the fighting, he told me his family's home had been burned to the ground.

The driver took me to inner Colombo, where I was able to find an inexpensive hotel. It was in an old part of the city with sooty, grimy buildings made of cut stone, built during the colonial days of Great Britain's rule. Dark-skinned men and women in sarongs and saris moved slowly through the narrow cobblestone streets. Oxcarts out numbered automobiles, and the cries of children rose in the hot sticky air. I loved it: the sights, sounds, and smells of an Asia so new and different.

That first night in Colombo I slept the restless sleep of a jet-lagged traveler, awaking the following morning as the first light crept into my room. Dressed in soft white linen draw-string pants and a matching shirt, I walked out to explore the city. The streets were almost deserted; an oxcart or two rumbled softly along. Vendors stood on street corners with steaming pails of milk. Thin-armed old men in rags swept the street with brooms made of long twigs. A *chai* (tea stall) opened up and I sat on the curb of the street drinking sweet tea as the warm sunshine fell upon my shoulders.

After tea I walked down a small lane between old brick buildings where I came upon a Hindu temple. I removed my shoes and entered, walking barefoot through the marble-floored chambers. The sweet smell of patchuli and jasmine incense was intoxicating, but at the same time it had a soothing effect. Worshippers in sarongs and saris sat in front of brightly colored ten-foot statues of Krishna, Ganesh, and Shiva. A shaft of light fell through an open window onto a woman in white who prostrated herself on the marble floor, her arms outstretched before her. From each of her hands petals of purple flowers spilled at the feet of Lord Krishna.

Coming back from the temple in the early light, I felt calm and peaceful. Near my hotel I came upon six people sleeping on the pavement, wrapped in blankets. I stopped and lingered, and as I passed, I bent down and dropped forty cents onto one of the sleepers. He sat up quickly. He was about my age, dark-skinned, and my first impression was of a deep intelligence. In perfect English he said, "Hello. Good morning." Then he asked me my name and why I had come to Sri Lanka. I told him I was called Ethan, that I was a student of Buddhism from America, and that I wanted to see his country. He smiled and said he was a Buddhist too. He asked me to sit down with him, which I did, and for forty-five minutes we talked while the other men and women sitting close by listened. The man's name was Bala.

Bala and I spent the next four days together in Colombo. He was a good companion for a stranger to have, and he eagerly showed me the sights of the city, especially the many temples and monasteries. Our favorite was a temple at Kaleniya, where according to local history the Buddha came by boat to settle a dispute between two warring clans. When the Buddha brought the clans to their senses, they became friends; as a gift, they offered the Buddha a gem seat. Bala explained the gem seat was still inside the crypt of the temple at Kaleniya.

On a hot sticky morning I checked out of my hotel and prepared to leave the city, heading for the hill country on a rented motorcycle. My plan was to spend the next month and a half traveling from village to village. Bala came to the back of the hotel and helped me load my knapsack onto the motorcycle. He showed me how to get out of the city on the least congested roads. When it was time to go, we gave each other an affectionate hug and bowed slowly to one another. Into my hand he placed a small ivory statue of the Buddha.

Getting out of the city in the traffic was a nightmare. Speeding cars and trucks made suicidal passes to overtake oxcarts, elephants, and old men herding their flocks of sheep and goats. Horns blared and black diesel smoke belched from hundreds of lumbering buses. There was no center line; people drove where they thought they could get through. Anger, frustration, and aggravation was in everyone's eyes. It was the worst driving I had ever experienced—far worse than Kashmir's, which still gave me bad dreams. And I was wrong to think that once out of the city the traffic would abate. It continued for miles along the main road to Kandy. For five hours I perservered, coming close to death on a number of occasions, until I reached Ambepussa, where, thank God, my motorcycle broke down.

When I found myself directly in front of a serene-looking guesthouse, I had every reason to believe that God was leading me there. It was a large, five-columned colonial home. I parked my motorcycle by the side of the road and walked up a tree-lined driveway to the veranda, where a man without shoes in a crisp white sarong and white shirt greeted me in a friendly, articulate voice. "Shall you be having tea with us?" He introduced himself as Sarat, the manager of the guesthouse. When I said yes, he ushered me to a table on the terrace under the leafy branches of a giant mimosa tree. While having tea and sandwiches, I gazed overhead where birds sang in the branches and onto the lawn below, where children played with small white goats. It felt wonderful to be off the road.

After tea I asked Sarat about accommodations. He told me he had six rooms in the attached annex, most of which were vacant. A newly converted government-run guesthouse, it was still unknown to most tourists. Sarat showed me his best chamber, an immaculately clean room with a high-ceiling fan and a bed with a white canopy of mosquito netting. The floors were smooth-tiled and covered with grass mats. The small attached bath had modern plumbing and a shower, and outside there were gardens and a patio with a table and chair. The room was six dollars a night and included breakfast and dinner.

That evening, after a rest and a shower, I ate on the terrace of the guesthouse beside a handful of French tourists and Sri Lankan businessmen. I was particularly interested to see that the local men ate

Morning bathers, Ambepussa

with their fingers. When I asked Sarat if he thought it would be improper for a westerner to do the same, he laughed and said he hoped I would. The two young waiters brought small dishes of curried lamb and chutney, rice with garlic and chili sauce, and pickled vegetables on small tin plates. At first try I was uncomfortable balling up the gooey rice and eating the greasy lamb with my fingers, but by the end of the meal I had overcome my self-consciousness. The French guests looked askance.

Sarat came by at the end of the meal, and we chatted for a while about why I had come to Sri Lanka. When I told him I was interested in traditional and rural villages, he said I should take a walk in the morning on the mud pathways behind my room, adding he did not think I would be disappointed with what I found.

In the early morning, as the sun was coming over the mountains, I walked out slowly, like a young child coming upon a new-found garden. Villagers in sarongs and saris bathed in streams along the trail. The women were extremely beautiful, and I tried not to stare as I passed. The valley opened up into a broad sweep of green rice paddies that stretched for a mile. In the soft light of morning, village men and women were at work in knee-deep water separating rice plants. Oxcarts moved along the fringe of the valley. A handful of orange-robed monks walked briskly under black umbrellas. At the far end of the valley the rain forest rose up to the spine of the mountains, where small thatched houses were spread out beneath the canopy of coconut trees. In the first light of the sun, three white temples glistened halfway up the mountain.

I crossed the valley on narrow, slippery mud paths, sometimes no wider than six inches, slipping occasionally into the brown water. The villagers harvesting their rice let my bungling go unnoticed and greeted me instead with warm smiles and pidgin English expressions that were delightfully out of place. "Hello Mister, I am fine." "Why is your country?" "You are a clever man." I said good morning and bowed slightly, wondering if I, too, were committing some social blunder.

At the far end of the valley I took a narrow wooded trail to a promontory where I sat in the sunshine eating bananas I found growing along the path. When I turned to stand up and continue on, I found a handful of boys in sarongs staring at me. They were perfectly motionless and silent, grinning broadly. I smiled at them and wished

On the path to school

them good morning. One boy called out to me as if he was reciting his English lesson: "Hello, Mister. I am fine. Where are you? Good-bye. Thank you." Then the children laughed and soon lost their self-consciousness. They circled around me and touched my skin and stared up at my blue eyes with amazement.

A twelve-year-old boy with a bicycle offered to drive me down to the rice paddies on his handlebars. I accepted, but wondered why I had when I found myself unpleasantly perched on the uncomfortable things. I warned him I did not want any accidents, but he only laughed as he pushed off with his feet. Soon we were speeding down the bumpy trail, careening around sharp corners, forcing old men and women, cats and dogs, chickens, and even an oxcart loaded with grain to pull to the side as we whizzed by. Tears streamed down my face, making the scenery blurred and chaotic. I shouted and screamed for the boy to put on his brakes, but he laughed. Finally at the bottom of the hill we coasted onto the flats. I was laughing now, as was the boy, and when the bike lost all its momentum, we fell over sideways onto the ground. "But why didn't you put on your brakes and slow us down?" I asked him. He turned to me with the most caring eyes and said simply, "No brakes."

When I returned for breakfast at the guesthouse, I knew that the motorcycle's breaking down in Ambepussa had been perfect for me. It was exactly the kind of village I was looking for. When I asked Sarat to place a call to Colombo to have the motorcycle agency come up and repossess the machine, I could see he was happy. I suspected few tourists ever noticed this village.

For the next week I took morning and afternoon walks through the countryside visiting with people who expressed—in limited English—their appreciation for my interest. They seemed surprised that someone from the United States had come to visit them. During the heat of midday I rested in my room, shades drawn, the ceiling fan circulating the hot humid air. When I confided to Sarat that I felt a little weak, he laughed and told me it took two weeks to become acclimated to Sri Lanka's temperatures.

At the end of the first week I asked Sarat if he thought I would look foolish if I wore something cooler and more comfortable than my blue jeans, perhaps a sarong like the men in the village wore. He said it would be a most fitting thing to do, adding that he had been going to

Mother and child

166 *Ambepussa*

suggest this to me.

As Ambepussa did not have any sarong shops, I was forced to board a bus for the nearby trading center of Warakopola. The buses were horribly outdated old barges, great lumbering crates that belched black smoke as they inched along. As I boarded and paid my fifteen cents to the driver, I averted my eyes, for what I knew was coming. I began to walk to the rear of the bus, trying to appear as nonchalant as possible. Blue jeans, too-long hair blowing about, white, blue-eyed, I raised my eyes slowly and saw the whole bus smiling at me. I smiled back and sat down on the nearest seat, next to an old bare-chested and toothless man in a loose-fitting loin cloth who held a mesh sack with three coconuts. He grinned and patted the seat with his hand to welcome me.

Warakopola was a busy crossroads town with a population of several thousand people. It sat on the main road to Kandy, the capital of the hill country, where most of the tourists went. In Warakopola open stalls and small shops displayed local produce. Inexpensive tools for sale lay about on the ground. Merchants hawked their wares, and vendors sold delicious-smelling street food (such as skewered shish kabob) that always tempted me, but which I inevitably refused, following the advice of vagabonding books that urged caution with street food.

I found a lavender sarong that pleased me and purchased it from a Muslim merchant who was deeply intrigued by my decision to go native. He even gave me a discount on it and folded his arms, smiling as I stuck it under my arm and caught a bus for Ambepussa. When I got home, I asked the staff if they could show me how to wear my sarong. The two young waiters, Ravinda and Rahula, and the old laundry man came out from their quarters and showed me how to wrap it around my waist. They also showed me how to hoist it up if I ever had to run to catch a bus or dash through mud puddles.

That evening when I came into the dining room, I tried to walk with the grace and aplomb of the Sri Lankan men: barefoot, proud, and serene. As I walked past several of the staff, I could feel their eyes on me and hear them whispering about my new sarong and white shirt, my bare feet, and my hair (slicked down with a little oil). When Ravinda put down my ice water and butter dish, he commented with quiet dignity, "Very nice, suh."

Everyone wanted to meet me, and everyone, in his own way, wanted to be hospitable to a visitor who had come to spend time in his village. When I had the time and energy, I enjoyed meeting them—human beings reaching out toward a stranger from afar. But often, when I became tired or uncentered, the overload was staggering. Once I fell asleep in a clump of grass under some palm trees in the forest. When I awoke, I slowly realized that several villagers stood around in a circle silently staring at me. I felt like Gulliver.

As I walked through the hillsides inspecting new wildflowers and butterflies and watching the iridescent blue and white kingfishers dart over the rice paddies, I usually came upon a house I had never seen before. Often the mother and father, and sometimes the old grandparents, stood by the path hoping for a visit. I loved the sound of their English; even more I loved their warm hearts. "Oh, suh, come please, please come, come, come have tea." And if I then swung down the trail and took off my day pack, great excitement unfolded. Father got out the best chair in the house and patted the seat encouragingly. Mother made a small hearth fire and brewed fresh tea. A son scampered to the top of a palm tree and returned with a ripe coconut which the father cut open. A sister would scavenge in the forest for ripe jackfruit.

Their homes were neat and clean—simple thatched cottages made from local mud bricks. Almost everyone in the village worked small plots in the rice paddies. Some harvested white latex from small stands of trees on the hillsides. A few families had factory-made chairs and tables and wood-framed glass display cases with a few revered plates and dishes. But usually their homes were without much adornment. People slept on the floor on grass mats and ate their rice or millet cooked on an open-hearth fire.

Because conversations were difficult for most of the villagers, I often showed them things from my knapsack that were immediately and easily understood. They all enjoyed a scrapbook I had brought of my family in New England—especially snapshots of my son Taylor playing baseball or riding his motorcycle and of my three blond nieces swimming at the beach. And everyone loved the pictures of winter in New England: skating and skiing shots that made their eyes roll. If the opportunity presented itself, which it usually did, I always tried to pass out some of the highly-prized needles I had brought with me (eight

Old man digging irrigation ditch

hundred, to be exact). After a mother had taken time to give me tea, or a father had whacked off the top of a ripe coconut for me to drink from, I would pull out a packet of assorted needles and ask the family to choose three.

In the early morning I liked to practice zazen meditation in the three white temples on the hill. The white wall of my room in the guesthouse could have easily served me, but I found a power and a calming presence in those ancient shrines. The temples were small buildings of cut white stone that housed the traditional Buddhist artifacts of the village: wall hangings and murals depicting the life of Buddha, bronze and stone statues of the Buddha, an assortment of bells, clothbound sacred texts, and altars with lighted candles. In the largest of the temples there was a ten-foot wooden statue of Lord Buddha painted fiery carousel colors. I sat on the smooth marble floor in the half-lotus position in front of the statue and meditated for forty-five minutes. Back straight, eyes half closed, hands held palms up at the navel, I practiced quieting my mind. During the first week of my stay, the children of the village used to come to the temple and watch me, pressing their faces against the window. Their giggling distracted me as much as my own monkey mind.

After a time their fascination wore off. Later, as I approached the temple for my morning meditation, they often waited for me along the trail in silence and handed me flower petals to sprinkle at the feet of Buddha.

The monastery below the temples was the home of seven monks, young men in their late teens and early twenties. The grounds surrounding the monastery were filled with spacious gardens and tree-lined lawns. I loved watching the shadows fall about the monastery in the late afternoon, and the orange-robed monks walking with each other as they inspected young fruit trees or flower beds. We saw each other from time to time. Our communion with one another was always simple and direct: a smile, a slight bow, sometimes a flower given.

I grew fond of a diminutive eleven-year-old monk with a shaved head and sparkling eyes. He was in charge of the temple keys and usually opened and closed the doors for me. The first time I saw him, I knew he was special. He was very simple and authentic. When he walked through the gardens and bent to smell a flower, or when he

The little monk

stopped and patted a dog on its head, he was completely absorbed in those actions. He was the closest thing I have ever experienced to a living Buddha. Every time I saw the little guy, I wanted to run up and hug him and run my hand over his smooth head. But I knew that would be totally out of place and highly irreverent. When he took me to the temple and unlocked the door to let me meditate in the morning, I touched my forehead to the hem of his robe, which was the custom.

There was a small stone building down by the rice paddies called the Bodhi House. It was a simple mud-and-thatch structure with open windows that looked out to the white temples in the mountains. It belonged to the entire village, a place where people could take refuge from the sun or rain and be quiet by themselves. Rising above the small house was a large bodhi tree (the same tree species under which the Buddha gained enlightenment). I used to love spending time at the Bodhi House, lying on the cool earth floor, gazing up through the open doorway at the sky and clouds, listening to the wind in the leaves. It was a haven, a place which by its very design and association with the Buddha seemed to encourage me to look for my own simplicity and authenticity.

At the request of some school teachers, I often stopped at the small schools that dotted the valley. My favorite was a primary school close to the temples. I stopped there whenever I could. Small boys in crisp blue shorts and girls in white jumpers sat on a smooth log in the sunshine. When the teacher saw me passing by, she called and asked me to give an English lesson. I said one word or phrase or sentence and the children repeated it back to me in their singsong voices. Their favorite word was "frisbee," which cracked them up every time they said it. One day I brought them my own frisbee and taught them to play.

Across the main road from the guesthouse was a district of the village called Danowita. It was a poorer area than the community encompassed by the broad valley of rice paddies. The people of Danowita worked mud and straw into bricks for the village houses. They were especially fond of having me photograph them, and whenever they saw me coming along the worn pathways of the jungle they lined up in a group with hopeful expressions on their faces. I tried as often as I could to stop and visit with them and make formal portraits.

174 *Ambepussa*

The Poddyappuhamy family in front of their store

Ambepussa had a small store in the jungle that I tried to frequent at least once a day. Local produce was unloaded from oxcarts that came up from Warakopola: bananas, coconuts, mangoes, potatoes, pineapples, sacks of rice, millet, barley, spices, herbs, and fresh vegetables. Women came by during the day with eggs, fresh butter, and cheese in baskets balanced on their heads. From time to time an elephant could be found at the store. It was used to haul big loads such as cement blocks and tin for a villager's cottage and roof. In addition to the produce the store featured some glass jars with candy and gum, and a few tins of condensed milk. The store was owned by a young couple named Podyappuhamy and Rosilyn. Their three little daughters were my best young friends in the village: Eenoca, 8; Taranga, 6; and Baby, 3.

Every day the old men of the village gathered at the store. There were usually eight or ten regulars, bare-chested and dressed in colorful sarongs with their white hair tied back in neat small buns. Whenever I came, one of the old men inevitably climbed up a tall coconut tree and brought down a fresh coconut for me to drink from. Others often treated me to a fresh mango or pineapple. Almost every one of them tried to teach me to enjoy chewing the *arica* they so dearly loved. In a wooden pestle they ground up the nuts, added a dollop of lime, a touch of local tobacco, and wrapped the concoction in a green leaf. This they loved to chew, and this, they assumed, was what I wanted to chew. Each time I tried all eyes were on me. Most of the time I swallowed a bit of the tart mixture and nearly choked to death, much to the gentle, discreet laughter of the hopeful old men. But I never gave up trying.

On the path that wound from the monastery back to the rice paddies I often ran into an English-speaking villager by the name of Grayson. He came home over the mountains from the school in Mirigam where he taught English, his books in one hand, a walking staff in the other. He was about my age and wore western clothing: blue jeans, a button-down shirt, and sneakers. He was appreciative of my having come to Ambepussa as he enjoyed speaking English and especially enjoyed hearing American idioms like "far out," "wow," or "out of sight." He desperately wanted to get out of Ambepussa and live in Germany or England or the United States. We shared many evenings at his house in the mountains, where we sat out under the stars drinking locally brewed beer and talking late into the night.

One day Grayson told me he wanted me to meet a sadhu, or holy aspirant, who was living in a cave above his house in the mountains. I told him I would enjoy it, particularly as we did not have too many sadhus back home. The following afternoon we climbed high up to where we saw smoke curling from a small cave in the cliffs. We called out a greeting and climbed the last hundred yards on a steep trail. The sadhu was waiting at the mouth of the cave when we got there. He was a young man, perhaps in his early twenties, with matted dread-locks. He wore an orange loincloth and nothing more. He had a wild and argumentative look on his face, and he ushered us into the cave quite brusquely.

Inside we sat on grass mats. Above him on a wooden shelf were a few tins of dried milk and a rusty skillet. At his feet he kept a small fire going. The cave had a sour smell to it, and there was litter in the corners. Almost at once the man asked me why I was studying Buddhism. I told him that I respected the Four Vows of the Buddhist: to liberate all beings, to uproot endless blind passions, to penetrate the gates of truth, and to attain Buddhahood. With Grayson as inter-preter, the man launched into something of a harangue. He spoke at length about the path that he was on, stressing time and time again that his teacher practiced the only correct form of Buddhism. All others were wrong. He added that if I did not accompany him to meet his teacher I was a fool. Forty-five minutes later he came to the end of his diatribe, a talk that reminded me of myself fifteen years earlier, when I had tried to convince friends my guru was the perfect master of the universe. When we left him and walked out into the brilliant late afternoon light, the mountain breeze, the birds singing, and the deep blue color of the sky seemed extraordinarily beautiful and poignant—as close to the truth the sadhu and I were striving for as anything a teacher could bestow.

One of the things I liked about being in Asia was the opportunity to interact with severely deformed or maimed people in everyday situa-tions. When I rode the bus down to Warakopola, I often encountered a teenage boy with the most severe cleft palate I had ever seen. Where his nose should have been, two long fangs jutted out. His mouth was split up the center. When I first saw him getting on the bus, I avoided his face. But each time after that I began to see that the boy himself accepted his disfigurement. His eyes twinkled, and in his own way he even smiled—sometimes at me. Near the end of my stay I was able to sit next to him and look squarely at his face without turning away. It was a strong lesson for me.

There was another young boy in Ambepussa who similarly inspired me to see my problems were small in comparison to his. He was a ten-year-old who lived without family at the base of the mountains. No one in the village knew much about him. I encountered him on two different occasions, and both times he was playing in the leaves by himself. He was unable to walk upright. He had thin mangled legs that did not work correctly and he moved about like a monkey on all fours. His hands were turned backward. He slithered across the leaf-covered floor of the forest with great speed and dexterity, dragging a soiled gunnysack in which he apparently kept a few things. On both occasions I stopped to talk to him. His English was virtually incomprehensible, but his bright eyes, his smile, and his endearing face were a joy and a wonder to behold. I gave him a little money each time and left him as I had found him, playing by himself like a spider in the leaves.

I frequently visited the Jayasiri family. Sarat was pleased I had met them and explained that they were one of the more prosperous and progressive families in the village. Jayasiri and his wife Premadasa and their four teenage daughters lived in a new house near the guesthouse. It had a tile roof and polished wooden floors and was one of the very few to have electricity. Jayasiri was nearing fifty. He was tall and lithe and dressed immaculately in a white sarong and shirt, his hair well oiled and short-cropped. He was outgoing and spoke good English. I liked him the very first time I met him along the path. He kindly invited me home for dinner on the following evening.

When I arrived at Jayasiri's house at dusk, the yellow light of sunset streamed onto the stone patio where his beautiful wife and four daughters stood waiting for me. They were dressed in pink and white saris, their long black hair tied in neat braids. The girls giggled as I approached. One burst past the others and introduced herself as Wasantha and asked if I had brought my camera (which I had) and wondered if I could take some pictures. Jayasiri soon appeared and I made formal portraits of the entire family.

The women of the family served Jayasiri and me tea on the porch as we talked about the rice harvest. Soon after, we sat down at the dinner table where Wasantha and Premadasa quietly waited on us, as was the custom of the village. We were served chilled red melon with crushed black pepper, stewed jackfruit, manioc with a curry gravy, and for dessert, sweet black tea and small cakes. At the end of our meal Jayasiri asked if I would like to attend the full moon celebration (*pansa*), at the temple on the following Saturday. I told him I would be delighted to go with him.

A week later, during a soft warm rain that fell for hours, Jayasiri appeared at my room. It was a long way to the temple, and we walked under his umbrella in the downpour without any conversation. For me the sounds of the night were too wonderful to interrupt with idle talk. I think Jayasiri felt the same way. Tree frogs croaked loudly as we made our way under leafy branches along the path. The streams gurgled as they raced down the hillsides. Our bare feet made squishy sounds in the soft mud. And from time to time a great gust of wind sounded in the trees overhead.

When we arrived twenty minutes later, a congregation of thirty or more villagers were waiting patiently for us under the protective eaves of the largest temple. Each carried a small candle cupped in his hands, and the reflected light illuminated each face. Old men in white loin-cloths leaned up against the temple walls. Grandmothers with gray hair looked out at the mist and rain. The small boys and girls I had taught in school stole smiles from me.

Soon after our arrival, a small brass bell was rung by the boy monk I liked so much. From a sheltered alcove each person began to pass his lit candle on to the next person. I was at the end of the line, and with Jayasiri quietly guiding me, I placed each candle on the altar inside the largest temple. Shortly incense sticks were passed along, and I placed these too on the altar. A second bell was rung and everyone came into the temple and sat on the floor. The little monk began to recite *gatas*, and for about half an hour we chanted these ancient Buddhist prayers. I did not understand any of the words, and yet I felt close to the others, filled with a sense of peace and joy.

On the way home Jayasiri and I stopped at Podyappuhamy and Rosilyn's store, where we rested out of the rain with a handful of old men and women who were also returning from the ceremony. Podyappuhamy gave us a sugar and flour confection and smiled affectionately at me. Taranga, Eenoca, and Baby came out and sat on the counter and let me play "This Little Pig Went To Market" with them.

The little monk with a friend
on temple steps

Often I simply stayed in my room and read or wrote in my journal or sunbathed in the garden. From time to time I liked to wander down to the guesthouse and talk with the staff. I especially liked to visit the two waiters whose manners at mealtimes were so humble and dear that I felt I should serve them when I visited them in their dirty and disheveled little quarters in the basement of the building.

My favorite person at the guesthouse was the old laundry man, Gamal, a toothless eighty-year-old who always wore baggy shorts and went about without shirt or shoes. I used to bring him my laundry twice a week. Often I sat on the floor at his feet and watched as he put coals from his small fire into the iron to heat it.

Gamal was an old Buddha. He washed and ironed my sarong and shirts as if he were preparing the laundry for the Lord himself, so sure, exacting, and proud was he of his craft. He was not flashy or witty, like the cooks, who used to chase me around the kitchen when I asked for a snack. And he was not wise in the same sense that Sarat was wise, about religion or bus schedules or the history of his village. But he was simple and well-worn and did what he did attentively and with deep reverence. When Gamal brought my shirts and sarong back to me, he knocked on my door. I opened the door and found him standing there in his worn baggy shorts looking at me with a calm face as he proudly held the laundry in his arms.

Gamal rarely spoke. Often a small smile was on his lips. He proved to be a great teacher. Back home, when my friends asked me what Buddhism was like in Sri Lanka, I told them about Gamal.

I loved walking through the rice paddies at the end of the day when white egrets walked through the lush green reeds. I often went to sit on the steps of the Bodhi House and imagined I was living centuries ago. One night at sunset I saw the figure of a woman on the other side of the valley. She was waving at me. I waved back. Slowly the figure moved higher along the path toward the forest. Was it the beautiful young woman I photographed yesterday at the water hole, the woman who brought water in a brass jug across the wooden bridge? We were a long way off but could still see each other in the lingering light. We waved at short intervals. She got smaller and smaller. Each time we waved we became more excited. We were expressing a strong emotion at a very long distance. When the inevitable last wave came, just before

A young monk at the village temple

184 *Ambepussa*

she entered the forest, we jumped and waved with both arms back and forth. Then she was gone. And for a short time nothing moved in the entire valley.

During my final day I went to the temples for the last time and prayed at the feet of the Buddha. The small monk came out and our eyes met. We smiled at one another. Podyappuhamy and Rosilyn gave me fruit. One old man presented me with an *arica* nut to chew on. With Baby in tow, Eenoca and Taranga held my hands and walked me to the edge of the paddies. Jayasiri and Premadasa waved as I made my way to the guesthouse.

At the guesthouse I had a final tea and walked around the gardens that had been my home for the past few weeks. Sarat, Ravinda, Rahula, and the cooks came out to say good-bye, standing in a line, admiration in their eyes. I went to each, saying thanks and giving each a small gift of money. Gamal appeared in his baggy shorts and stood as he always stood, content. He grinned as I gave him his gift. Then I was gone, heading down the tree-lined path on which I had arrived.

Designed by Edmund Helminski
Typeset in Palatino by Stevens Graphics
Printed on Warren's Lustro Gloss, an acid-free paper,
by the Murray Printing Company

Ethan Hubbard's photographs were developed
by Linda DeMellier and by Jerry Fish